BRAIN BENDERS

for CHAMPIONS

CROSSWORDS, LOGIC PUZZLES, WORD GAMES & MORE

EDITED BY STANLEY NEWMAN

PUZZLE
WRIGHT
PRESS
New York

PUZZLE WRIGHT PRESS

New York

An Imprint of Sterling Publishing
1166 Avenue of the Americas
New York, NY 10036

ISBN 978-1-4549-1264-4

Distributed in Canada by Sterling Publishing
℅ Canadian Manda Group, 664 Annette Street
Toronto, Ontario, Canada M6S 2C8
Distributed in the United Kingdom by GMC Distribution Services
Castle Place, 166 High Street, Lewes, East Sussex, England BN7 1XU
Distributed in Australia by Capricorn Link (Australia) Pty. Ltd.
P.O. Box 704, Windsor, NSW 2756, Australia

For information about custom editions, special sales, and premium and
corporate purchases, please contact Sterling Special Sales at 800-805-5489 or
specialsales@sterlingpublishing.com.

Manufactured in China

2 4 6 8 10 9 7 5 3 1

www.puzzlewright.com

CONTENTS

Introduction
4

Meet the Puzzles!
5

Meet the Authors
9

Puzzles
10

Answers
201

Introduction

Welcome to *Brain Benders for Champions*, a colorful cornucopia of puzzle varieties. The 300+ puzzles herein were first published by Reader's Digest as part of its highly successful *Mind Stretchers* book series, for which I served as the original puzzle editor. As such, they were sold by mail-order invitation only, so it is a great pleasure for me to make them available now to you, as part of the "retail" puzzle audience.

As you might expect, there are plenty of America's two most popular puzzles herein: crosswords and sudoku. But there's much more—including many varieties of word puzzles, arithmetic puzzles, and logic puzzles, not to mention mazes and other eye-catching visual challenges. The bigger puzzles are arranged in order of difficulty, with the most gentle (marked with a single star) appearing first, with the stars gradually increasing up to the knottiest five-star challenges at the end. The smaller bottom-of-page puzzles are all pretty much of medium difficulty throughout.

Of course, you'll find all the answers in the back of the book, just in case.

If you enjoy this book, I invite you to continue the fun with the other volumes in the series. For their help in the preparation of this book and its puzzles, I would like to thank:

- Neil Wertheimer, my editor at Reader's Digest, and Harold Clarke, who first introduced me to Neil
- The other principal puzzle authors (alphabetically): George Bredehorn, Conceptis Puzzles, Dave Phillips, and Peter Ritmeester
- Sandy Fein, who assisted in the editing and compilation of these puzzles as originally published and for this edition
- At Puzzlewright Press: Peter Gordon, Francis Heaney, and Jon Delfin, for their diligent handling of all the publishing details

Your comments on any aspect of this book are most welcome. You can reach me via regular mail at P.O. Box 69, Massapequa Park, NY 11762 (please enclose a self-addressed stamped envelope if you'd like a reply).

If you're Internet-active, you can reach me electronically through my website: StanXwords.com. StanXwords.com features puzzlemaker profiles, solving hints, and other fun stuff for crossword fans. Please drop by for a visit.

Best wishes for happy solving!

—Stanley Newman

Meet the Puzzles!

The wide range of puzzles in this *Brain Benders* book includes both classics and innovative varieties you're likely not to have seen before. New to you or not, here are instructions, tips, and/or samples for each puzzle type.

WORD GAMES

Crossword Puzzles
Edited by Stanley Newman

The 60 crosswords in this book are presented in order of difficulty. The one- and two-star puzzles have straightforward clues and answers that are everyday words. As we add stars later in the book, you'll find a somewhat broader vocabulary, but most of the added challenge comes from less obvious and trickier clues. What you won't find are uninteresting obscurities such as "Village in Macedonia" and "Kentucky Derby winner in 1906."

Clueless Crosswords
by George Bredehorn

These 7-by-7 grids have no clues, but need none. Based on the letters filled in for you, find the unique set of common uncapitalized seven-letter words that will complete the puzzle.

Example **Solution**

Hints: Examining the filled-in letters, you should be able to determine a few additional letters early on, or at least make some good guesses! Of course, as in standard crosswords, the task gets easier as more letters are written in.

Split Decisions
by George Bredehorn

In this puzzle, technically also a "clueless crossword," each answer consists of a pair of words whose spellings are the same except for two consecutive letters. For each pair of words, the two sets of different letters are already filled in for you. All answers are common words; no phrases or hyphenated or capitalized words are used (unless specifically noted). Certain missing words may have more than one possible solution, but there is only one solution for each word that will correctly link up with all the other words.

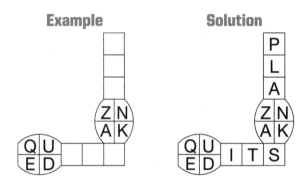

Example **Solution**

Hints: Look at the shorter (three- and four-letter) words first, because there will be fewer possibilities that spell words. In each puzzle, there will always be a few such word pairs that have only one possible solution.

Triad Split Decisions
by George Bredehorn

This puzzle is solved the same way as Split Decisions, except you are given three letters for each word instead of two.

Example **Solution**

Sudoku

by Conceptis Puzzles

Each sudoku puzzle is a 9-by-9 square grid, split into nine square regions, each containing nine cells, with some of the cells filled in. You must fill in the rest of the cells with the numbers 1 to 9, such that no number appears twice in any row, column, or region. There is only one correct solution for each puzzle.

Example

8	4						7	1
3			7	1	8			9
	5	9		3	6			
	9	7	8		1	2	3	
	6							9
	3	1	2		9	7	6	
		4	3		2	9		
1			5	9	4			6
9	8						5	3

Solution

8	4	9	6	2	5	3	7	1
3	2	6	7	1	8	5	4	9
7	1	5	9	4	3	6	8	2
5	9	7	8	6	1	2	3	4
2	6	8	4	3	7	1	9	5
4	3	1	2	5	9	7	6	8
6	5	4	3	8	2	9	1	7
1	7	3	5	9	4	8	2	6
9	8	2	1	7	6	4	5	3

Hints: The given numbers will enable you to rule out cells where certain numbers cannot appear. For example, if there is a 3 in a cell, a 3 cannot appear in the same row, column, or region. By examining the numbers present at any stage, you will be able to determine where additional numbers must go.

Hyper-Sudoku

by Peter Ritmeester

Peter is the inventor of this unique sudoku variation, which includes four additional 3-by-3 square regions (indicated by gray shading) in which the numbers 1 to 9 will each appear once.

Example

1	4	5	9			7		
		7	5	8	4	1		
3				7	2		5	
5	9		4	2	7			
	6		8					7
	7	4				2	9	5
	1						8	
	5		2			6		
6			7			5		

Solution

1	4	5	9	3	6	7	2	8
9	2	7	5	8	4	1	3	6
3	8	6	1	7	2	9	5	4
5	9	3	4	2	7	8	6	1
2	6	1	8	5	9	3	4	7
8	7	4	6	1	3	2	9	5
7	1	9	3	6	5	4	8	2
4	5	8	2	9	1	6	7	3
6	3	2	7	4	8	5	1	9

Find the Ships

by Conceptis Puzzles

In this pencil-and-paper variation of the board game Battleship, a group of ten ships of varying sizes must be placed into the grid. Some "partial ships" may be filled in to get you started. Complete the puzzle according to these rules:

1. Ships are oriented horizontally or vertically, never diagonally.
2. A ship will never appear in a box with wavy lines, which indicates open sea.
3. The numbers on the right and bottom of the grid tell you how many squares in that row or column contain parts of ships.
4. Two ships will never touch each other, not even diagonally.

Example   Solution

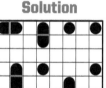

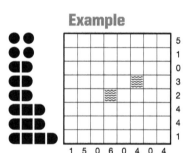

Hints: Solving involves both finding squares where ships must go and eliminating squares where ships cannot go, which you can cross out. You can always cross out all squares in any row or column marked with a 0. If you know a particular square will be occupied by a ship, even if you don't yet know what size it is, you can cross out the squares that are diagonal to it—none will ever contain a ship.

ABC

by Peter Ritmeester

In this somewhat sudoku-like logic puzzle, you must figure out where the three letters A, B, and C go in each row, knowing each row and column in a completed puzzle contains exactly one A, one B, and one C—with the remaining squares blank. The clues outside certain rows and columns indicate the first letter encountered when moving in the direction of an arrow.

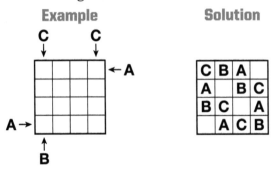

| Example | Solution |

Hints: Never assume that the first letter encountered must go in the first square. The first square (or first two squares, in larger grids) could be blank. A good way to start is to look for places column and row clues intersect (for example, when two clues look like they are pointing at the same square). At times, it's possible to figure out where a letter goes by eliminating every other square as a possibility for that letter in a particular row or column.

Fences
by Conceptis Puzzles
Fences are sort of a "do-it-yourself maze." Connect the dots with vertical or horizontal lines so a single loop is formed with no crossings or branches. Each number in the grid indicates how many lines surround it; squares with no number may be surrounded by any number of lines.

Hints: First, fill in the links (the spaces between pairs of dots) you are certain about, and then figure out how those links must be connected. Also, mark off any links that can't be connected. These include all four links around each 0. Another good starting step is to look for any number 3 next to a 0, for which you can fill in the links around the 3 immediately. Looking at the four corners and groups of adjacent squares with numbers filled in is often helpful. In any case, the links that you fill in will enable you to see patterns that should allow you to complete the puzzle.

Number-Out
by Conceptis Puzzles
Your task in this puzzle is to eliminate numbers by shading squares so that no remaining number appears in any row or column more than once. Shaded squares may not touch each other horizontally or vertically, and all unshaded squares must form a single continuous area.

Example

5	3	1	4	3
4	5	3	4	2
2	1	2	3	4
1	3	2	1	4
3	4	2	5	4

Solution

5	3	1	4	3
4	5	3	4	2
2	1	2	3	4
1	3	2	1	4
3	4	2	5	4

Hints: Any square between a pair of the same numbers must always be unshaded, so if three of the same number are consecutive in a row or column, the one in the middle must be unshaded, and other two must be shaded. (You can circle unshaded numbers as a reminder.) Once you shade in a square, you know that the squares adjacent to it, both horizontally and vertically, must be unshaded. Any numbers that are unduplicated in their row and column will never be shaded.

Star Search
by Peter Ritmeester

This is a first cousin to Minesweeper. You must find the stars hidden among the blank squares, using the numbered squares, which indicate how many stars are hidden in squares adjacent to them (including diagonally). There is never more than one star in any square.

Example

Solution

Hint: If, for example, a 3 square is surrounded by four empty squares, but two of those squares are both adjacent to the same 1 square, the other two empty squares around the 3 must contain stars.

123
by Peter Ritmeester

Each 123 grid contains domino-like pieces with three numbers. You must fill in each blank square so each "domino" contains one each of the numbers 1, 2, and 3, according to these rules:

1. No two horizontally or vertically adjacent squares can contain the same digit.
2. Each completed row and column of the grid must have an equal number of 1's, 2's, and 3's.

Example

Solution

Hints: Any blank square that is adjacent to two different numbers must contain the third number, by Rule 1. Rule 2 becomes useful later in the solving process. Knowing that, for example, a 9-by-9 diagram must have three 1's, three 2's, and three 3's in each row and column allows you to use the process of elimination to deduce what the blank squares in nearly filled rows and columns must be.

VISUAL PUZZLES

Throughout *Brain Benders for Champions* you will find many unique mazes, visual conundrums, and other colorful challenges developed by maze master Dave Phillips. Each comes with unique instructions and will require its own approach to solving. Our advice for each is the same, though: Be patient and persevere!

In addition, you will find these other visual puzzles:

Line Drawings
by George Bredehorn

The goal of each Line Drawings puzzle is different, but the task is always the same: Figure out where to place the prescribed number of lines to partition the space in the instructed way.

Hint: Be sure to use a pencil and a straightedge as you work. Some lines come very close to the items within the region, so being straight and accurate with your line-drawing is crucial.

One-Way Streets
by Peter Ritmeester

The diagrams in these maze-like puzzles represent streets on which a road rally (starting at A and ending at B) is taking place. Black squares are checkpoints. You must find a route that starts at A, passes through all checkpoints exactly once, and ends at B. (Harder puzzles use S's to indicate "start" and "stop," and don't tell you which is which.) Arrows indicate one-way traffic for that block only. No intersection may be entered more than once.

Example   ### Solution

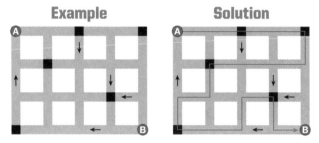

Hints: The arrangement of checkpoints and arrows will limit the possibilities for the first and last checkpoints passed, so you'll probably find it helpful to work from both the start and end of the route. Also, keep in mind that the placement of an arrow on a block doesn't necessarily mean that your route will pass through that block. You can also use arrows to eliminate blocks where your path will not go.

BRAIN TEASERS

More than 150 short brain teasers, most by book editor Stanley Newman (except as noted) supplement the puzzles described above. Each includes instructions and an example. You'll find the following types scattered throughout:

Addition Switch*	Small Change
Betweener	Sound Thinking
Century Marks	Sudoku Sum*
Choice Words	Think Alike
In Other Words	Three of a Kind*
Initial Reaction	Transdeletion
Mixagrams**	Two-by-Four
National Treasure	Who's What Where?
Say It Again	Wrong Is Right

  * by George Bredehorn
** invented by and cowritten with
   George Bredehorn

MEET THE AUTHORS

STANLEY NEWMAN (editor of this book and puzzle author) is crossword editor for *Newsday*, the major newspaper of Long Island, New York. He is the author/editor of over 200 books, including the autobiography and instructional manual *Cruciverbalism* and the best-selling *Million Word Crossword Dictionary*. Winner of the first U.S. Open Crossword Championship in 1982, he holds the world's record for the fastest completion of a *New York Times* crossword—2 minutes, 14 seconds. Stan operates the website www.StanXwords.com, where a new Newsday Crossword can be found every day—from the medium-difficulty Sunday, to the gentle challenges of Monday and Tuesday, to the Saturday Stumper, generally acknowledged to be the most challenging crossword in American newspapers today.

GEORGE BREDEHORN was a retired elementary school teacher from Wantagh, New York. His variety word games appeared in the *New York Times* and many puzzle books and magazines. Every week for more than 20 years, he and his wife, Dorothy, hosted a group of Long Island puzzlers to play some of the 80-plus games that George invented.

CONCEPTIS PUZZLES (www.conceptispuzzles.com) has been offering the most advanced logic puzzling experience in all media since its debut in 1997. Presently, more than 20 million Conceptis puzzles are solved each day in newspapers, magazines, books, and online, as well as on smartphones and tablets across the globe.

DAVE PHILLIPS has designed visual puzzles for books, magazines, newspapers, PC games, and advertising for more 30 years. In addition, Dave is a renowned creator of walk-through mazes. Each year his corn maze designs challenge visitors with miles of paths woven into works of art. To enjoy more of Dave's mazes, please visit www.mazefanatics.com.

PETER RITMEESTER is chief executive officer of PZZL.com, which produces many varieties of puzzles for newspapers and websites worldwide. Peter has also been general secretary of the World Puzzle Federation. The Federation organizes the annual World Puzzle Championship, which includes difficult versions of many of the types of logic puzzles that Peter has created for this book.

★ Silent Signals by Gail Grabowski

ACROSS

1 Guys-only party
5 Rodeo rope
10 Con game
14 Coupe or sedan
15 Hunter constellation
16 Make simpler
17 Long division word
18 Rural water sources
19 Suffix with "major"
20 Fanciful sleeping place
22 High-class tie
23 Fishing vessels
24 Old Iranian ruler
25 Cairo's country
27 Protective shoreline structure
30 Rabbit relatives
31 Hitchhiker's digit
33 Very small
34 Airport landing stat.
35 Swiss miss of fiction
36 Rural hotel
37 Wet ground
38 Thaws
39 Rock concert groups
41 Unique
43 Pulls suddenly
44 Bygone days
45 Scenic sights
47 Approximately
49 Powerful ocean surge
53 Hawaiian necklaces
54 Difficult puzzle
55 Wicked
56 Copenhagen citizen

57 Courtroom event
58 Thorny flower
59 ___ and crafts
60 Restless
61 Did laps in a pool

DOWN

1 Go yachting
2 Sandwich fish
3 Business letter abbr.
4 "Farewell!"
5 Like 1% milk
6 "You ___ kidding!"
7 Farm storage buildings
8 Real estate sign
9 Light switch settings
10 Playground fixture
11 Get some sleep
12 Concerning
13 Run into
21 "I dropped it!"
22 Moby Dick pursuer
24 Highway hauler
25 Completely consume
26 College average component
27 Lather
28 Advances, as money
29 Camera part
30 Skirt borders
31 Spill the beans
32 Top tune
35 Furnace output

38 Atomizer output
39 Cry loudly
40 Responds to
42 Brings about
43 Every 12 months
45 Drop in on
46 Creative thoughts
47 Alan of *M*A*S*H*
48 Winnie-the-Pooh, e.g.
49 Shredded
50 Declare openly
51 Traveler's document
52 Pertaining to grade school: Abbr.
54 School support org.

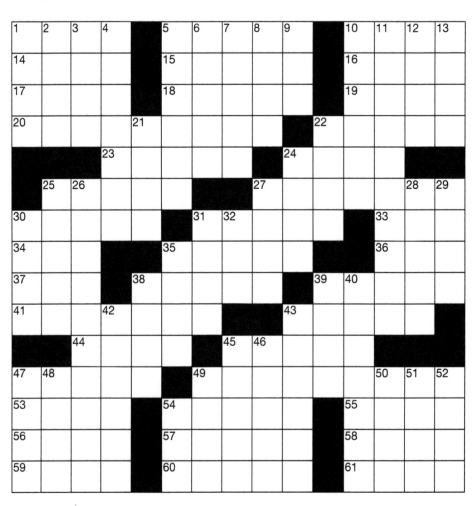

★ Falling Leaves

Which of the fallen leaves is in the middle of the pile? (That is, which has the same number of leaves below it as above it?)

CENTURY MARKS

Select one number in each of the four columns so that the total adds up to exactly 100.

For example:
$$\frac{6}{\boxed{8}} + \frac{\boxed{15}}{73} + \frac{\boxed{40}}{61} + \frac{29}{\boxed{37}} = 100$$

$$\frac{22}{11} + \frac{11}{40} + \frac{31}{18} + \frac{45}{20} = 100$$

Fill in the blank squares so that every row, column, and 3×3 box contains the digits 1 through 9 exactly once each.

			6			1		
					3			8
	9	8	5	7				4
6			1				4	5
7	1			5			3	9
5	2				9			6
8				9	1	6	5	
3			4					
		7			5			

M I X A G R A M S

Each line contains a five-letter word and a four-letter word that have been mixed together. (The order of the letters in each word has not been changed.) Unmix the two words on each line and write them in the spaces provided. For example, D A R I U N V E T = DRIVE + AUNT. When you're done, find a two-part answer to the clue by reading down two letter columns in the answers.

CLUE: Ash, but not ember

A T H E W A D I N = _ _ _ _ _ + _ _ _ _

L A J O U G H T S = _ _ _ _ _ + _ _ _ _

A F O R M R O R E = _ _ _ _ _ + _ _ _ _

I D O D E D A L S = _ _ _ _ _ + _ _ _ _

★ Animal Acts by Sally R. Stein

ACROSS

1 Wood-cutting tools
5 Retired fast jets: Abbr.
9 Soup-serving utensil
14 Coup d'___
15 Winter outerwear
16 How some tuna is packed
17 Singer Fitzgerald
18 First chip, in poker
19 Roll with a hole
20 Chattering
23 Gloomy ___ (glum one)
24 Give the OK
25 Star of Bethlehem followers
27 Very energetic one
31 Not fooled by
34 Synagogue leader
38 Is in the red
39 Opposed to, to Li'l Abner
40 Verdi specialty
41 Brown shade
42 Milk mishap
43 Boyfriend
44 Work hard
45 Of little importance
46 Makes a mistake
47 Traveling, as a music group
49 "If ___ a Hammer"
51 Nap, in Mexico
56 Japanese money
58 Devouring
62 ___ cum laude (lesser honor than "summa")
64 Helper
65 Like a desert
66 Burglar, for one
67 Got taller

68 Home loan: Abbr.
69 Sharpshooter Oakley
70 Large bodies of water
71 Fresh talk

DOWN

1 "So long!"
2 Map book
3 Takes a stroll
4 Amount bet
5 Inadequate
6 Ballad, for example
7 "So long!"
8 Do a slow burn
9 Country west of Egypt
10 Santa ___, California
11 Shirking work
12 In ___ of (instead of)
13 Right-angled letters
21 Where New Delhi is
22 "Famous" cookie man
26 Run amok
28 "___ your life!" ("Forget it!")
29 Hang around for
30 "The Wizard of ___ Park" (Edison)
32 Pinball infraction
33 Merely
34 Judge's gown
35 Imitative sort
36 Having relevance to
37 Hair-grooming tool

42 Bit of parsley
44 Ruckus
48 *Time* rival, for short
50 Start the day
52 Dutch cheeses
53 Somewhat, slangily
54 Tiny tree branches
55 Chile's mountains
56 Community center: Abbr.
57 Have coming
59 Falls behind
60 Cannoneer's command
61 Brainstorm
63 "There's ___ in 'team'!"

Connect the dots with vertical or horizontal lines so that a single loop is formed with no crossings or branches. Each number indicates how many lines surround it; squares with no number may be surrounded by any number of lines.

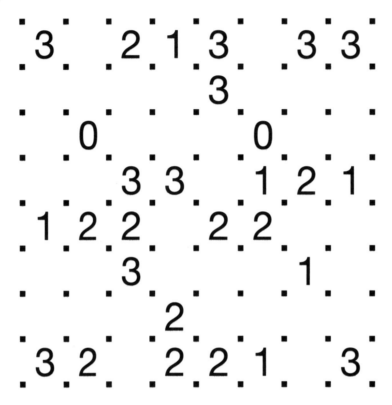

Initial Reaction

Identify the well-known proverb from the first letters of each of its words. For example:
L. B. Y. L. = Look before you leap.

F. I. F. _____

Wrong Is Right

Which of these four words is misspelled?

A) perchance

B) pervey

C) persnickety

D) perpetrate

★★ Line Drawing

Draw three straight lines from edge to edge, none crossing each other, to make four regions that each contain the same total amount of money.

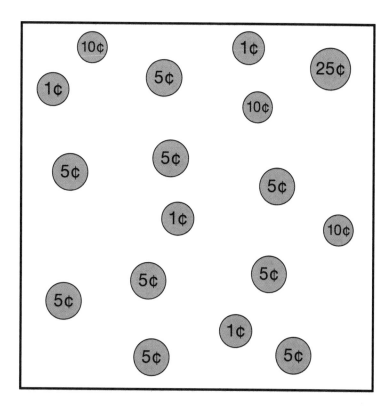

Three of a Kind

Find a set of three hidden words in the sentence that go together in some way. For example, "Chefs were **bus**ily slicing **car**rots and **cab**bage" conceals the set "bus, car, cab."

We eagerly reminisced about the old Latin years.

Who's What Where?

The correct term for a resident of Oakland, California, is:

A) Oaklandian   B) Oaklander

C) Oaklandite   D) Oaklie

★ Back to School by Sally R. Stein

ACROSS

1 Annoying one
5 Health resorts
9 Scarlett of *Gone With the Wind*
14 Region
15 Barn's upper space
16 Gains altitude
17 Weight-reducing plan
18 Skin care brand
19 Suspect's excuse
20 Shipped off
21 Finest-quality
23 Supposedly wise bird
25 "Electric" fish
26 Wide view
31 Elapsed
36 Australian bird
37 Make into law
39 Sandwich cookie
40 Got ready, as for a meeting
44 Matured
45 Couches in family rooms
46 Golf platform
47 Also-rans
50 Faraway forts
52 Ingest
54 Explosive initials
55 Mountain road warning sign
61 Army "lights out" tune
65 Largest artery
66 From the U.S.: Abbr.
67 Spiny houseplant
68 Substantial
69 Warsaw native
70 Toward sunset
71 Doubly curved letters
72 Lose traction
73 Tree-chopping tools

DOWN

1 Writing tablets
2 Cleveland's lake
3 Noticed
4 Art on some arms
5 Rightmost part of a highway
6 Horseback game
7 Worship from ___
8 Fashion
9 Fortuneteller
10 Battle of Bunker ___
11 Where Korea is
12 Some Civil War soldiers
13 Sale condition
22 Morning condensation
24 Small songbird
26 Accelerator or brake
27 Friend, in Spanish
28 Sculptor's subjects
29 Church service
30 Sneeze sound
32 At present
33 Horses' gaits
34 Artist's cap
35 Oxen connectors
38 Soybean product
41 Type of poem
42 Was important
43 Sports cable channel
48 Takes care of, as a debt
49 Droop
51 Canada's capital
53 Hidden obstacles
55 Identical
56 On one's ___ (alert)
57 Historical periods
58 Diminutive suffix
59 Run ___ (go wild)
60 Food shop
62 TV host Trebek
63 Prepare for a portrait
64 Movie studio stages

Shade squares so that no number appears in any row or column more than once. Shaded squares may not touch each other horizontally or vertically, and all unshaded squares must form a single continuous area.

4	1	4	3	1
3	4	4	2	5
1	1	2	5	3
5	5	5	1	3
5	2	3	4	3

Think Alike

Unscramble the letters in the phrase SAY YOKE to form two words with the same or similar meanings. For example, BEST RATING can be anagrammed to spell START and BEGIN.

_____   _____

In Other Words

There is only one common uncapitalized word that contains the consecutive sequence of letters ZAA. What is the word?

_____

Enter the maze from the top, pass through all the blue squares exactly once each, then exit, all without retracing your path.

Small Change

Change one letter in each of these two words to form a common two-word phrase. For example, PANTRY CHEW becomes PASTRY CHEF.

SHOP BID

_____

ACROSS

1 Football official
4 Brazilian ballroom dance
9 Groom's companion
14 Letter after kay
15 Be of use to
16 Baseball great Hank
17 Playpen item
18 *Leaving Las Vegas* star
20 Likely
21 Calendar squares
22 Game with kings and pawns
23 Uses the microwave, maybe
25 Chilled, as champagne
26 Author ___ Stanley Gardner
27 Rocks that are mined
28 Long-term S&L investments
31 Adjust, as a telescope
33 Golf instructors
34 Loafer or moccasin
35 On the peak of
36 Tilts
37 Kitchen flooring piece
38 Unruly event
39 Cereal grains
40 Mom's sisters
41 Sixth sense: Abbr.
42 24-karat
43 Sicilian volcano
44 Work hard
45 First New Testament book
48 Runs away
50 Postage-paid enclosure: Abbr.
51 Numero ___
52 Implement with ink
54 Tongue-clucking sound

55 Proofreader's find
56 Well-built
57 Pool stick
58 ___ board (manicurist's tool)
59 Country singer Buck
60 Barnyard bird

DOWN

1 Pave again
2 Marry secretly
3 Depart abruptly
4 Summer footwear
5 Pilot a plane
6 *Miracle on 34th Street* store
7 Life stories, briefly

8 The whole shebang
9 Huge parties
10 Competed in the Indy 500
11 Keogh alternatives
12 Dalmatians and dobermans
13 U-turn from WSW
19 Means of approach
24 Blow, volcano-style
25 Gets the wrinkles out of
27 Make a speech
28 Cabinet for fine dishes
29 Oaf
30 Catches a glimpse of

31 Price for a cab ride
32 Soul singer Redding
33 Oyster product
34 Daredevil's feat
36 ___ May Alcott
40 Goes to, as a concert
42 Prose counterpart
43 Enter cautiously
44 Male operatic voice
45 Syrup flavor
46 Come next
47 Roused from sleep
48 Document to fill out
49 Entice
50 Winter precipitation
52 Lawyer's charge
53 Prefix for metric

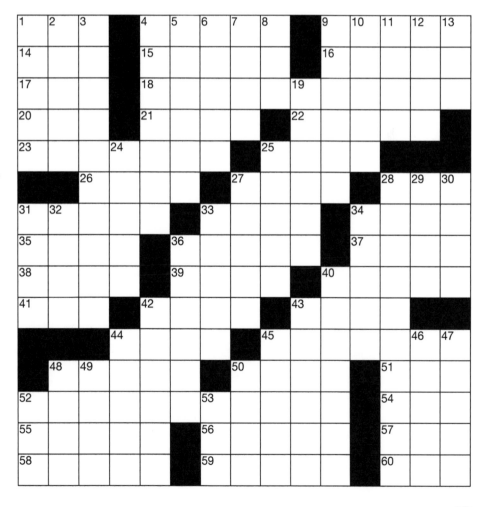

★ One-Way Streets

The map below represents a set of intersecting streets on which a road rally (starting at A and ending at B) is taking place. The black squares represent checkpoints. You must find a route that starts at A, passes through all checkpoints exactly once, and ends at B. Arrows indicate one-way traffic for that block only. No intersection may be entered more than once.

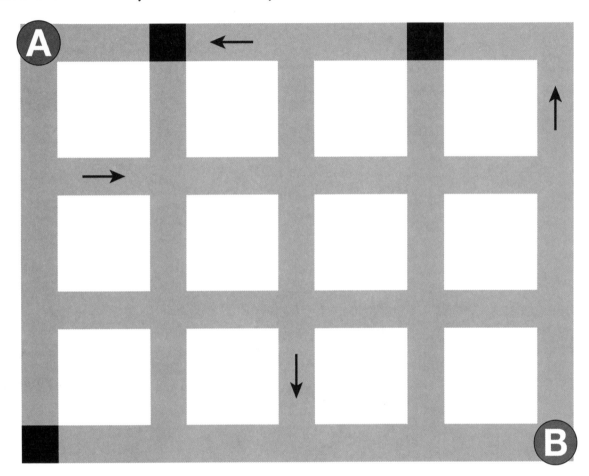

Sound Thinking

Common words whose consonant sounds are M and N (once each, in that order) include MINE and MINNOW. The longest such word has seven letters. What is it?

_____

In this crossword puzzle with no clues, each answer consists of two words whose spellings are the same except for the pairs of consecutive letters given. All answers are common words (no phrases), and none are hyphenated or capitalized. Some individual clues may have more than one solution, but only one word pair will correctly link up with all other word pairs.

Transdeletion

Delete one letter from the word SENATE and anagram the rest to get a grammatical term.

_____

★ Star Search

Can you find the stars hidden in some of the blank squares? Numbered squares indicate how many stars are hidden in the squares adjacent to them in any direction (including diagonally). There is never more than one star in any square.

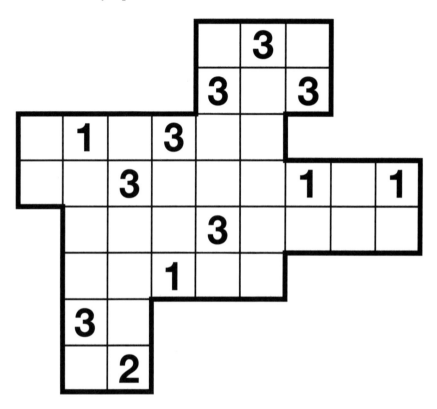

★ Serve and Protect by Gail Grabowski

ACROSS

1 British fellow
5 Hidden stockpile
10 Surrounded by
14 Ear part
15 False name
16 Competing team
17 Skeptic's remark
18 Finger or toe
19 Was sure of
20 Law enforcement vehicle
22 At the present time
23 Spud
24 Tart-tasting
25 Drops, as prices
28 Party planner
31 Wipe the chalk from
32 Pulls with force
34 Circus routine
35 Winery tub
36 Pie serving
37 Female deer
38 And so on: Abbr.
39 Hula skirt material
40 Play segment
42 Brought back to the payroll
44 Divvied up
45 Read, as a bar code
46 "And Jill came tumbling ___"
48 Saw socially
50 Highway barrier
54 Radiant quality
55 Backyard barrier
56 Capital of Norway
57 Guys-only party
58 Poker pot fees

59 Lean slightly
60 Wish earnestly
61 Bird houses
62 Talk back to

DOWN

1 Cut out, as coupons
2 Boxcar rider
3 Brother of Cain
4 Small dress sizes
5 Military school students
6 Wonderland girl
7 Humidor item
8 Barber's expertise
9 Superlative suffix
10 Invite to dinner
11 Telepathic one
12 Creative thought
13 Like grass in the morning
21 Show concern
22 Prepare, as a salad
24 Shoe bottom
25 Crowbar, e.g.
26 Make a speech
27 Band on a timepiece
28 Affectionate embraces
29 Tea biscuit
30 Knight's horse
32 Lettuce unit
33 Classifieds, for example
36 Small songbird

39 Class reunion attendee
40 Storage building
41 Vegetable soup ingredients
43 Glacial era
44 Emphasize
46 Family members
47 Aspect
48 Short race
49 Coupe or sedan
50 Hackman of Hollywood
51 China's continent
52 Misfortunes
53 Real estate parcels
55 Ceiling appliance

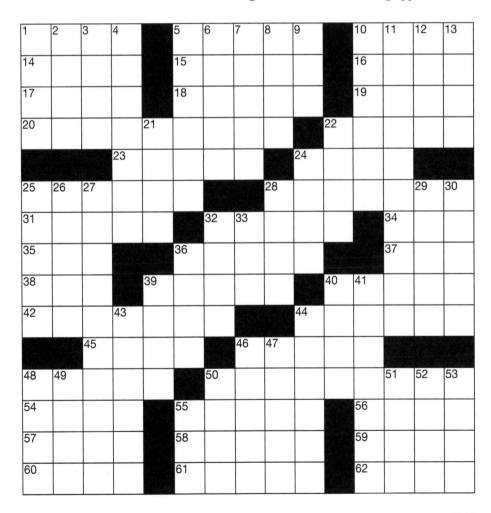

Fill in the blank squares so that every row, column, 3×3 box, *and* each of the 3×3 gray regions contains the digits 1 through 9 exactly once each.

						2		6
			6		5		7	
		3	2				8	4
		1	8				4	9
	4			9	6			2
9	2			1	7	5	3	8
		9	1	2		4		
	8	5						3
1		2			3		9	

Each line contains a five-letter word and a four-letter word that have been mixed together. (The order of the letters in each word has not been changed.) Unmix the two words on each line and write them in the spaces provided. For example, D A R I U N V E T = DRIVE + AUNT. When you're done, find a two-part answer to the clue by reading down two letter columns in the answers.

CLUE: Tofu

C A P A B I C E N = _ _ _ _ _ + _ _ _ _

F A S T E R N U N = _ _ _ _ _ + _ _ _ _

S E X P A C T R Y = _ _ _ _ _ + _ _ _ _

A G O D N E R D S = _ _ _ _ _ + _ _ _ _

Fill in the diagram so that each rectangular piece contains the digits 1, 2, and 3 once each, according to these rules: 1) No two horizontally or vertically adjacent squares can contain the same digit.
2) Each completed row and column of the diagram must have an equal number of 1's, 2's, and 3's.

2			3		
					2
		3			
	3			2	

S U D O K U S U M

Fill in the missing digits from 1 to 9 so that each is used once and the sum of each row and column is as indicated.

Example:

	12	14	19
6			3
17	6		
22		8	

Answer:

	12	14	19
6	1	2	3
17	6	4	7
22	5	8	9

	15	12	18
18		3	
8			5
19	7		

★ Housework by Sally R. Stein

ACROSS

1 ___ in the neck (pest)
5 San Antonio landmark
10 Swiss mountains
14 Loosen, as a necktie
15 "Hearty appetite!"
16 "Billy" beast
17 Pants accessory
18 Perch
19 Be jealous of
20 Major overhaul
23 "No ___, ands, or buts!"
24 Miami clock setting in Jul.
25 Most up-to-date
29 Places for pillows
31 Distress signal
34 Soprano's gig
35 By oneself
36 Lose brightness
37 Gabbing about the good old days
40 Tehran's country
41 Evaluate
42 ___ beef (sandwich meat)
43 Fractions of a gal.
44 Sows and boars
45 Tops of waves
46 Assist
47 Highway warning
48 After-bath skin soothers
56 Short skirt
57 Showed on TV again
58 Neck of the woods
59 Zealous
60 Give a lecture
61 Fail to attend
62 Go out with

63 Aroma detectors
64 Tabbies and terriers

DOWN

1 British taverns
2 All over again
3 Off from work
4 Short letter
5 Aimless
6 Tamer's beasts
7 Wide-eyed
8 Catchall category: Abbr.
9 Exactly
10 Actor's representative
11 Before ___ (soon)
12 Install a sidewalk
13 Home for 44-Across
21 One living near the Leaning Tower
22 Commercials, for example
25 What no Mensa member has
26 Not together
27 5-Across's state
28 Ireland nickname
29 Footwear for skiers
30 Otherwise
31 Long stories
32 Writer of praiseful poems
33 Religious groups
35 Hosiery mishap

36 Chunk of Arctic ice
38 Football field
39 Robin Hood weapon
44 Peach center
45 Biological copies
46 All kidding ___
47 Sudden outpouring
48 Hard-to-please star
49 Curriculum section
50 Infamous Roman emperor
51 Mardi ___
52 Slightly wet
53 A Great Lake
54 Take a break
55 Back talk
56 Fit to be tied

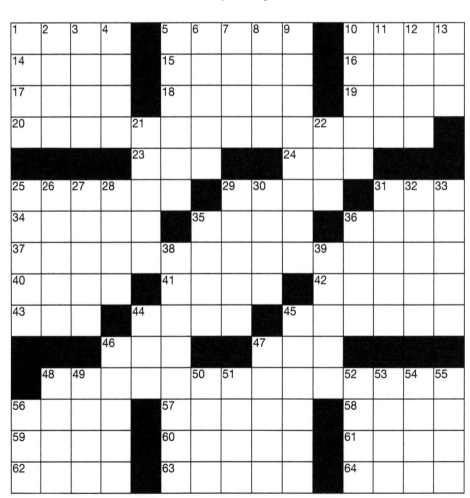

Enter the letters A, B, and C into the diagram, filling in some (but not all) of the squares so that each row and column contains each letter exactly once. The letters outside the diagram indicate the first letter encountered in the indicated row or column when moving in the direction of the arrow from that side of the grid.

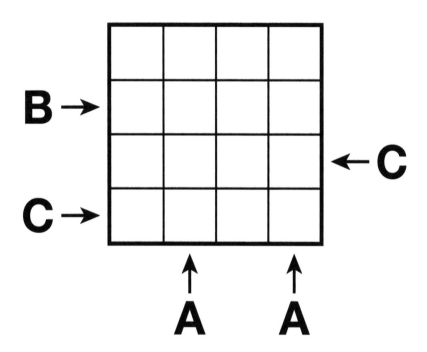

CLUELESS CROSSWORD

Complete the crossword with common, uncapitalized seven-letter words, based on the letters already filled in for you.

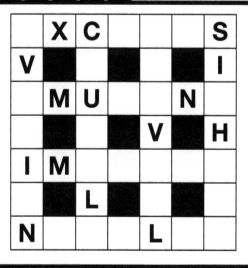

Ten ships of four different sizes (shown below left) are hidden in the diagram. Ships may be oriented horizontally or vertically, and may not touch each other, not even diagonally. A square containing wavy lines represents open water; such a square will not contain any part of a ship. Numbers at the edge of the diagram indicate how many squares in that row or column contain parts of ships, including any which may have already been placed as clues.

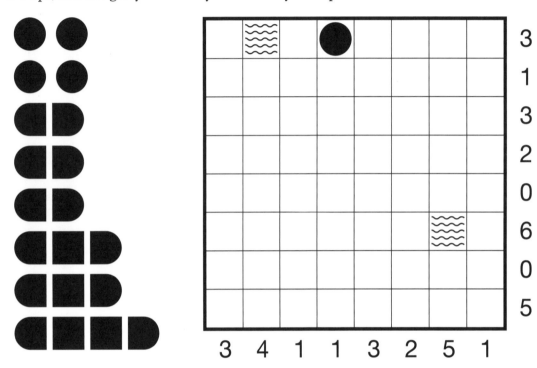

Betweener

What three-letter word can go between the two words below so that it forms compound words with both the word preceding it and the word following it?

ANY ___ ___ ___ **EVER**

Two-by-Four

The eight letters in the word VACANTLY can be rearranged in only one way to form a pair of common four-letter words. Can you find them?

___ ___ ___ ___   ___ ___ ___ ___

★ Cross That Bridge by Sally R. Stein

ACROSS

1 Bursts, as a balloon
5 ___ and dashes (Morse code symbols)
9 Studies hard
14 Neighborhood
15 Very frequently
16 Capital of Vietnam
17 Hope (for)
18 Impolite glance
19 Gold bar
20 Unimportant
23 Pluralizing letter
24 Sleeper's sound
25 Compete in a bee
27 Initially
31 "Alas!"
34 Nightclub routine
37 Seize
38 Radio studio sign
39 Performs as ordered
43 Informal eatery
44 Spilled the beans
45 ___ de Janeiro
46 Plumlike fruit
47 Shoe liners
50 Statement of belief
52 Tennis pro Monica
56 The A in NATO: Abbr.
58 *The Apprentice* boss
62 Providence, ___ Island
64 Chimney duct
65 Ancient Andes settler
66 Georgia city
67 Right away, in memos
68 Golden-___ (senior citizen)
69 "Omigosh!"
70 Speak in favor of
71 Onion relative

DOWN

1 Minor chess pieces
2 Hunter constellation
3 Green sauce
4 African desert
5 Painter Salvador
6 Designer Cassini
7 ___ the line (conformed)
8 Emphasize
9 Western South American nation
10 Jogged
11 Very thin spaghetti
12 Cow sounds
13 Makes use of a sofa
21 Racetrack patron
22 Pertinent
26 Touch down
28 Devotee
29 Eisenhower nickname
30 Relaxes
32 Short skirt
33 Therefore
34 Finds a sum
35 Spiral shape
36 Coffee break time, perhaps
38 Most peculiar
40 Crystal ball gazer
41 Scare word
42 Under the weather
47 Wedding phrase
48 Like skim milk
49 Soap opera, for example
51 Paradises
53 Sudden forward thrust
54 Banquet host
55 ___ plug (auto part)
56 Fighting force
57 Spicy Asian cuisine
59 Likewise
60 Waikiki feast
61 Company division: Abbr.
63 Female deer

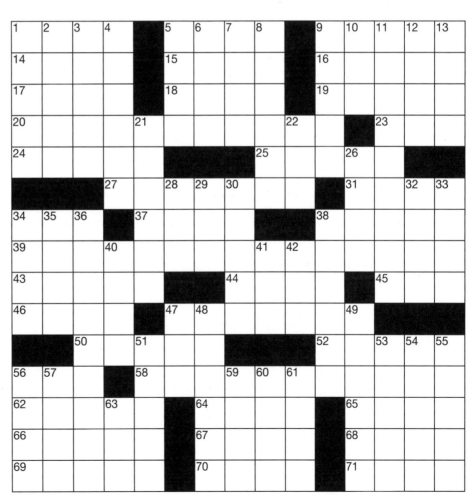

★ Flight Formation

Enter the maze from the left as indicated by the arrow, pass through all the stars exactly once each, then exit at right. You may not retrace your path.

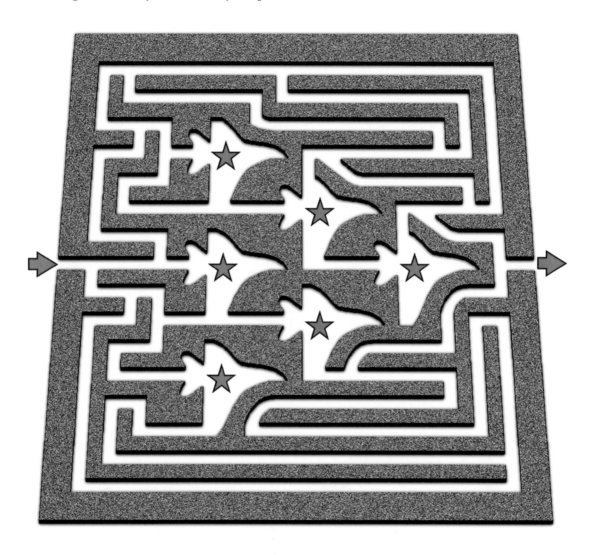

Small Change

Change one letter in each of these two words to form a common two-word phrase. For example, PANTRY CHEW becomes PASTRY CHEF.

HOG STAFF

_____

★ Fences

Connect the dots with vertical or horizontal lines so that a single loop is formed with no crossings or branches. Each number indicates how many lines surround it; squares with no number may be surrounded by any number of lines.

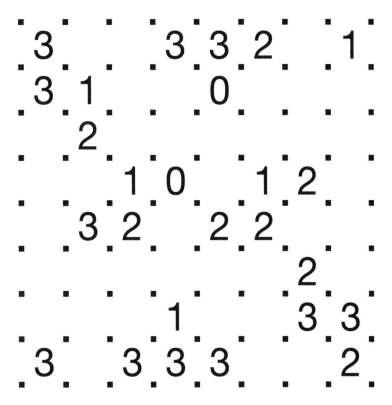

Initial Reaction

Identify the well-known proverb from the first letters of each of its words. For example:
L. B. Y. L. = Look before you leap.

L. B. B. B. _____

Wrong Is Right

Which of these four words is misspelled?

    A) sarsaparilla   B) sargeant

    C) sarcasm   D) sarong

★ Get the Door by Gail Grabowski

ACROSS

1 Post office purchase
6 Petty quarrel
10 Herbal brews
14 "You've got mail" addressee
15 Humdinger
16 Fire hydrant attachment
17 Nutritious snack
19 Condo division
20 One of a Capitol Hill 100: Abbr.
21 "___ the word" ("Don't tell anyone")
22 Topeka's state
24 Corn holders
25 Fuse, as metal
26 Cool and calm
29 Johnny Carson's successor
32 Married secretly
33 Overhead railroads
34 Huck Finn's transport
36 Be next to
37 Moose relative
38 Small taste
39 Ancient Roman's robe
40 Night bird
41 Orchards of orange trees
43 Cotton gin inventor Eli
45 Give in
46 Close by
47 Treaty
48 Nut in mixed nuts
51 Coupe or sedan
52 51-Across fuel
55 Creme-filled cookie
56 Wrestling hold
59 Grain storage structure

60 Breakfast chain, for short
61 New ___, India
62 Have a conversation
63 Church service
64 Strongboxes

DOWN

1 Droops
2 Pulled apart
3 Actor Alda
4 Fathers and grandfathers
5 Advance in rank
6 Shuts with force
7 London taverns
8 Pie ___ mode
9 Thanksgiving entrées
10 Stormy weather flash
11 Long periods of time
12 China's continent
13 Complete collections
18 Greased, as a 51-Across
23 Everybody
24 Peter Pan pirate
25 Take a stroll
26 Usher's offering
27 Arm joint
28 Bread maker's mixture
29 Toast topper
30 Too trusting
31 Repeatedly
35 Midterm or final
37 Wide-spouted pitcher
40 Just for the fun of it
41 Shred, as cheese
42 Writes down in a ledger
44 Driving range prop
47 Service station fixtures
48 Price to pay
49 Opera solo
50 Offer at retail
51 Cookiemaker Wally
52 Ernie Els's game
53 Feel sore
54 Glides on snow
57 "Now I get it!"
58 Meadow

★ Sudoku

Fill in the blank squares so that every row, column, and 3×3 box contains the digits 1 through 9 exactly once each.

3				1				7
	8		4	6			3	
6			9		8			1
		6		4		8	2	
9	4						6	5
	1	3		2		7		
1			3		2			8
	7			5	4		1	
4				7				9

M I X A G R A M S

Each line contains a five-letter word and a four-letter word that have been mixed together. (The order of the letters in each word has not been changed.) Unmix the two words on each line and write them in the spaces provided. For example, D A R I U N V E T = DRIVE + AUNT. When you're done, find a two-part answer to the clue by reading down two letter columns in the answers.

CLUE: Burn the midnight oil

S I L A N S H E W = _ _ _ _ _ + _ _ _ _

V I R O N S A D O = _ _ _ _ _ + _ _ _ _

P E R R U O R R R = _ _ _ _ _ + _ _ _ _

S W A L R E D E K = _ _ _ _ _ + _ _ _ _

Fill in the diagram so that each rectangular piece contains the digits 1, 2, and 3 once each, according to these rules: 1) No two horizontally or vertically adjacent squares can contain the same digit.
2) Each completed row and column of the diagram must have an equal number of 1's, 2's, and 3's.

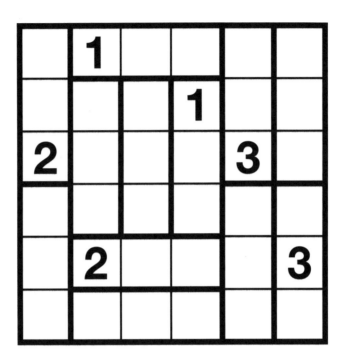

Who's What Where?

The correct term for a resident of Oxford, England, is:

A) Oxonian   B) Oxfordite

C) Oxforder   D) Oxfordian

Sound Thinking

There is only one common uncapitalized word whose consonant sounds are N, B, K, and L, in that order. What is it?

_____

★ For the Youngsters by Gail Grabowski

ACROSS

1 Makes mistakes
5 Some soda containers
9 Little rascals
13 Paperback, e.g.
14 Aroma
15 Egypt's capital
16 Attractive eyes, slangily
18 Nixon vice president
19 Opposite dir. from NNW
20 Breadbasket item
21 Crossword clue heading
22 Casual top
24 Goes in
25 Magazine execs: Abbr.
26 Less clear
27 Joint in the lower leg
30 Comes in last
31 Sphere
34 Installed, as carpet
35 Roadside lodging
36 Moisturizer ingredient
37 Advanced degree: Abbr.
38 Beach accessory
39 Jacket material
40 Scored, as a test
42 Coupe or convertible
43 Nimble-minded
44 Beach shelter
47 Urge onward
48 Topnotch
49 Physicians' org.
51 Vagabond
52 Water pistol
54 The Atlantic, for one
55 Go right or left
56 Bouquet holder
57 Hushed "Hey!"
58 Fill completely
59 Slow-cooked meal

DOWN

1 Recedes
2 Sunday dinner entrée
3 Terry cloth garments
4 Cloud's place
5 Red and green
6 Grownup
7 Christmas carol
8 Former jrs.
9 "Okay with me!"
10 Small part for an actor
11 Use a steam iron on
12 Female pigs
15 Desert plant
17 Groom's companion
21 Halo wearer
23 Grasped in one's hand
24 Artist's stand
26 Filled in a ballot
27 Swiss peak
28 Slangy refusal
29 Extreme gentleness, so to speak
30 Reduce, as a price
32 Fishing pole
33 Spelling competition
35 Fashion poser
36 Radiant quality
38 Pub
39 Cavalry sword
41 Say again
42 Dog or fox
43 Gators' kin
44 Judge's workplace
45 Constantly find fault with
46 Entertain
47 Stage accessory
48 Hue close to turquoise
50 Once more
52 Urban roads: Abbr.
53 "Plasma" appliances

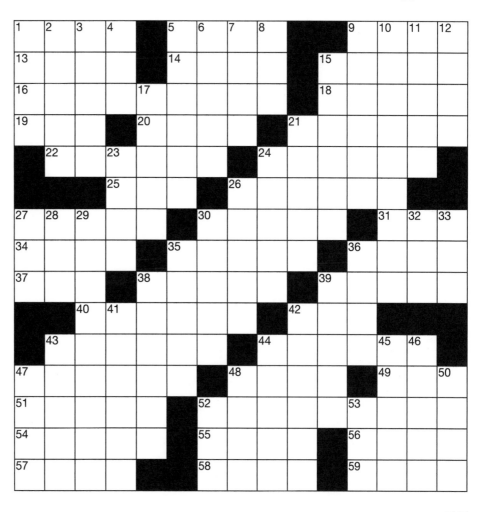

★ One-Way Streets

The map below represents a set of intersecting streets on which a road rally (starting at A and ending at B) is taking place. The black squares represent checkpoints. You must find a route that starts at A, passes through all checkpoints exactly once, and ends at B. Arrows indicate one-way traffic for that block only. No intersection may be entered more than once.

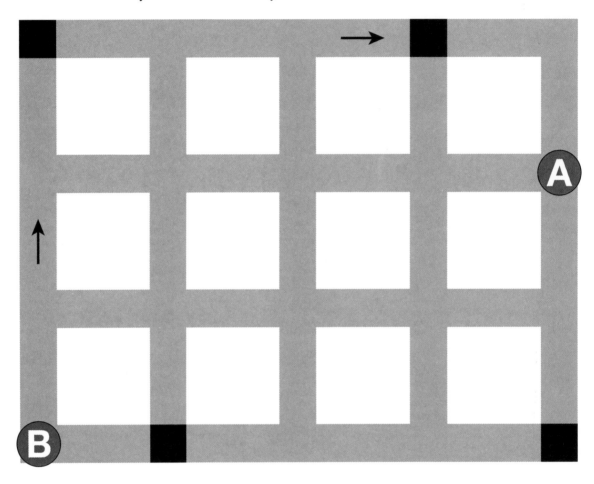

A D D I T I O N   S W I T C H

Switch the positions of two digits in the incorrect sum at right to get a correct sum. For example, in the incorrect sum 955 + 264 = 411, you would swap the second 1 in 411 with the 9 in 955 to get the correct sum 155 + 264 = 419.

$$\begin{array}{r} 186 \\ +694 \\ \hline 835 \end{array}$$

★ Missing Links

Find the three rings that are linked together, but linked to no others on the page.

Say It Again

What three-letter word can be either a type of mammal or a verb meaning "intimidate"?

—— —— ——

Can you find the stars hidden in some of the blank squares? Numbered squares indicate how many stars are hidden in the squares adjacent to them in any direction (including diagonally). There is never more than one star in any square.

		1	2	
2		4		
	3	4		1
2		3	3	2
				1
1	3		2	
	2			

CHOICE WORDS

Form three six-letter words from the same category by selecting one letter from each column three times. Each letter will be used exactly once.

Example: B A B C O T   Answer: BOBCAT, JAGUAR, OCELOT
         J O E U A R
         O C G L A T

         H E R H E R   _ _ _ _ _ _

         P A S A E S   _ _ _ _ _ _

         B O T T S R   _ _ _ _ _ _

★ Story Time by Sally R. Stein

ACROSS

1 Shouts of discovery
5 Male deer
9 "At what place?"
14 Army outpost
15 Opera solo
16 Propelled a rowboat
17 Hans Christian Andersen story
20 Ex–Supreme Court justice ___ Day O'Connor
21 College website suffix
22 Celebration
23 Parts of psyches
25 Many mos.
27 Blotter stains
32 Sheep herder of rhyme
37 College official
38 Part of the eye
40 Combine
41 House builders in a kids' story
44 Carrying a weapon
45 Prefix for graph or trooper
46 Edinburgh native
47 Security staffers
49 "Nyet!" sayers
51 Slangy agreement
53 Pro sports award: Abbr.
54 D-Day's conflict
58 ___ Baba
60 Shout of discovery
65 Grimm tale siblings
68 Nimble
69 Bright star
70 Flower stalk
71 Taxi device
72 Termination points
73 Change for a $20

DOWN

1 Behaves
2 Joke response
3 Prayer conclusion
4 Tater
5 Dressing ingredient
6 Give it a go
7 Assistant
8 Too showy
9 Chinese frying pan
10 Football game segment
11 Cleveland's lake
12 Take an apartment
13 Rim
18 Hold firmly
19 Sidewalk border
24 Piece of bacon
26 A portion of
27 Luggage attachment
28 Gandhi colleague
29 Fate
30 Sinister grin
31 Guitar relative
33 Coca-Cola rival
34 Author Jong
35 Incite
36 Bothersome ones
39 Play a guitar
42 Whirlpool
43 Casino city
48 Close tightly
50 Cowboy boot attachment
52 Wood-shaving tool
54 Sound of a punch
55 Salary
56 Monogram part: Abbr.
57 Tahiti or Maui
59 Get ___ the ground floor
61 Remainder
62 Suffix for kitchen
63 Sharp, as an appetite
64 Charitable donation
66 Always, in verse
67 Video store rental

Draw three straight lines from edge to edge to make five regions in which the letters in each can be rearranged to spell a word. Of the five words, none end in the same letter, and four are the same length.

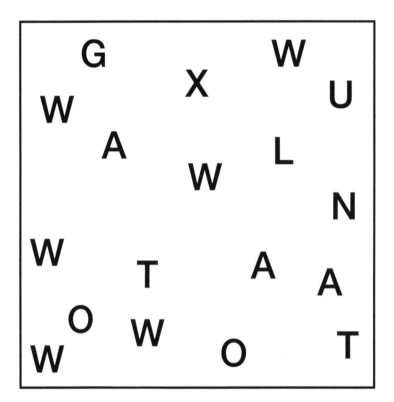

Three of a Kind

Find a set of three hidden words in the sentence that go together in some way. For example, "Chefs were **bus**ily slicing **car**rots and **cab**bage" conceals the set "bus, car, cab."

He scowled at the not-at-all tasteful jewelry.

In Other Words

There is only one common uncapitalized word that contains the consecutive sequence of letters VUN. What is the word?

_____

Enter the letters A, B, and C into the diagram, filling in some (but not all) of the squares so that each row and column contains each letter exactly once. The letters outside the diagram indicate the first letter encountered in the indicated row or column when moving in the direction of the arrow from that side of the grid.

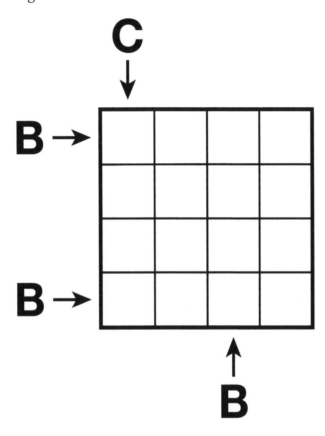

Two-by-Four

The eight letters in the word WHEEZING can be rearranged in just one way to form a pair of common four-letter words (besides WHEE and ZING, which don't require any rearranging). Can you find them?

__ __ __ __   __ __ __ __

★ Land Development by Gail Grabowski

ACROSS

1 Marked a ballot
6 Architect's design
10 24-hr. cash sources
14 In the know
15 Car
16 Sneaker, for example
17 Confidential scheme
19 Sentry's shout
20 Exclamation of disapproval
21 Church bell sound
22 Boulders
24 Cluttered condition
25 Peculiar mannerism
26 Bricklayers
29 Source of maple syrup
32 Most Jordanians
33 Aviator
35 "Roses ___ red ..."
36 Depend (on)
37 Pull apart
38 Ink smudge
39 NBC show with skits, for short
40 Stands in line
42 In need of tightening
43 Rural outing in a wagon
45 Mrs.'s husband
46 Discovers
47 Gooey hairdo holders
48 Black eye
50 Sailor's shout
51 Part of a minute: Abbr.
54 Accessories for suits
55 Sleeve feature on a sports jacket

58 Doing nothing
59 Observes
60 Hawaiian greeting
61 Scarlet and crimson
62 Pretzel topper
63 Train station

DOWN

1 Enormous
2 Has outstanding bills
3 Bulletin board fastener
4 Get something wrong
5 Becomes more profound
6 Dads
7 Temporary calm

8 From ___ Z
9 Uncertain
10 Off the ship
11 Words of appreciation
12 Burrowing mammal
13 Tennis match units
18 Dick Tracy's wife
23 Stadium level
24 ___-*Dick* (Melville novel)
25 Cotton swabs
26 Wetland
27 Sports complex
28 *Norma Rae* star
30 Got out of bed
31 Actor O'Toole
33 Fast food side order

34 Ignited
38 One in charge
40 Chianti or chablis
41 Line on an envelope
42 Frog's seat
44 Removes the suds from
45 Cat's cry
47 Haunted house spirit
48 Mix together
49 Stay out of sight
50 Brother of Cain
51 "That's enough!"
52 Canyon sound
53 Casual talk
56 Meadow
57 Pub beverage

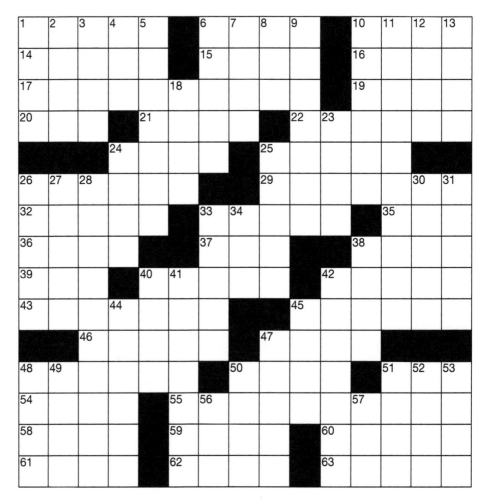

★★ Five by Five

Group the 25 numbers in the grid into five sets of five, with each set containing all the digits from 1 to 5. The numbers in each set must all be connected to each other horizontally or vertically.

Small Change

Change one letter in each of these two words to form a common two-word phrase. For example, PANTRY CHEW becomes PASTRY CHEF.

GOLD BELL

★ Find the Ships

Ten ships of four different sizes (shown below left) are hidden in the diagram. Ships may be oriented horizontally or vertically, and may not touch each other, not even diagonally. A square containing wavy lines represents open water; such a square will not contain any part of a ship. Numbers at the edge of the diagram indicate how many squares in that row or column contain parts of ships, including any which may have already been placed as clues.

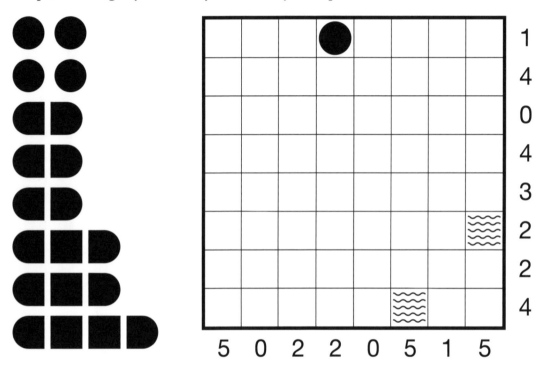

★★ Sudoku

Fill in the blank squares so that every row, column, and 3×3 box contains the digits 1 through 9 exactly once each.

9	5		1		4		7	8
		8				2		
	6		3		2		9	
2		5				7		9
				5				
8		1				6		3
	9		7		8		1	
		3				9		
7	8		2		1		3	6

M I X A G R A M S

Each line contains a five-letter word and a four-letter word that have been mixed together. (The order of the letters in each word has not been changed.) Unmix the two words on each line and write them in the spaces provided. For example, D A R I U N V E T = DRIVE + AUNT. When you're done, find a two-part answer to the clue by reading down two letter columns in the answers.

CLUE: Legit

S A F E M U B A D = _ _ _ _ _ + _ _ _ _

T I M A B O P S O = _ _ _ _ _ + _ _ _ _

A D M O I N G A L = _ _ _ _ _ + _ _ _ _

A D E M G A N G S = _ _ _ _ _ + _ _ _ _

★ It's for You by Sally R. Stein

ACROSS

1 Cheese with holes
6 Helper: Abbr.
10 Derbies and berets
14 Is compelled
15 West Coast sch.
16 Phrase of understanding
17 Stared at
18 Awl or chisel
19 River through Cairo
20 Have a good cry
21 Evasive language
23 Writer of praiseful poems
25 Brewed beverage
26 Merited
29 Weekend family excursion
33 Cook in the oven
34 Silly one
36 Exist
37 Wheeler-dealer
41 Compass pt. opposite WNW
42 Spiny houseplant
43 Signs of the future
44 "The Motor City"
47 Thinly scattered
48 Feel poorly
49 Irrigate
51 Open acting audition
55 Mid-March day
59 Don't include
60 Star soprano
61 Loud noise
62 One of Columbus's ships
63 Checkout counter unit

64 Prefix for violet
65 Biblical paradise
66 Infamous Roman emperor
67 "Here's to you!," for one

DOWN

1 Theater offering
2 Salary
3 Tropical spot
4 Go quickly
5 Pregrown grass
6 Sedans and coupes
7 Merit badge wearer
8 Messy one
9 Unlikely story
10 Allude to
11 Where Laos is
12 Spill the beans
13 Look for
21 Performed
22 Ending for puppet
24 Sandwich shop
26 Receded
27 Stand up
28 Thesaurus guy
29 Deal with adversity
30 Film critic, often
31 Removes creases from
32 In itself
34 Believed
35 Tic-tac-toe win
38 Submitted, as a contest entry
39 Lariat
40 Texas city
45 Wickerwork material
46 Lubricate
47 City in Mo.
49 Be unable to decide
50 San Antonio shrine
51 Dunce cap shape
52 In the thick of
53 Fork part
54 Give as an example
56 Statistics
57 Goes wrong
58 Usher's destination
61 However

★ Fences

Connect the dots with vertical or horizontal lines so that a single loop is formed with no crossings or branches. Each number indicates how many lines surround it; squares with no number may be surrounded by any number of lines.

```
  3  3  1        2

     2        0  3

           3        2

  3  3  2           2

  2           3  1  2

  3     2

     2  3        0

  3           1  2  3
```

Betweener

What three-letter word can go between the two words below so that it forms compound words with both the word preceding it and the word following it?

MID __ __ __ PORT

Wrong Is Right

Which of these four words is misspelled?

A) vibrate

B) celebrate

C) vertabrate

D) calibrate

In this crossword puzzle with no clues, each answer consists of two words whose spellings are the same except for the sets of three consecutive letters given. All answers are common words (no phrases), and none are hyphenated or capitalized. Some individual clues may have more than one solution, but only one word pair will correctly link up with all other word pairs.

Transdeletion

Delete one letter from the word ELDEST and anagram the rest to get a weather term.

_____

Fill in the diagram so that each rectangular piece contains the digits 1, 2, and 3 once each, according to these rules: 1) No two horizontally or vertically adjacent squares can contain the same digit.
2) Each completed row and column of the diagram must have an equal number of 1's, 2's, and 3's.

SUDOKU SUM

Fill in the missing digits from 1 to 9 so that each is used once and the sum of each row and column is as indicated.

Example:

	12	14	19
6			3
17	6		
22		8	

Answer:

	12	14	19
6	1	2	3
17	6	4	7
22	5	8	9

	13	14	18
19	8		
17			6
9		5	

★ Animalistic by Sally R. Stein

ACROSS

1 Book of maps
6 Units of current
10 Internet-based diary
14 Milk cows' home
15 Warsaw resident
16 Entice
17 Fond hope
18 Neighborhood
19 Actor Alda
20 Very ornery
23 Make a choice
24 Mine rock
25 Tiny rock
29 Former *Tonight Show* host
31 Weep loudly
34 British noble
35 Spanish rivers
37 Heaven-sent food
39 Very vain
42 Tailor, often
43 Fictional Karenina
44 Factual
45 Driver's licences, for example: Abbr.
46 Hankerings
48 More enormous
50 Arithmetic total
51 Actor Gibson
52 Very elusive
61 Ocean phenomenon
62 Actual
63 Charged at
64 Prayer's last word
65 Lass
66 Prefix meaning "tiny"
67 Musical tempo
68 Concludes
69 Frozen rain

DOWN

1 Finds a 50-Across
2 Sour-tasting
3 In ___ of (instead of)
4 Jordanian or Lebanese
5 H for hydrogen, for one
6 No longer together
7 Time after sunrise, poetically
8 Defendant's statement
9 Spring or summer
10 Hold responsible
11 Doozy
12 Of the mouth
13 Chromosome component
21 Pavarotti performance
22 Scent
25 Coke competitor
26 Golden-___ corn
27 Foreheads
28 Sky shade
29 Bank offerings
30 Sports cable network
31 Bull's sound
32 Punctual, as when saying a line
33 Cake creator
36 "No man ___ island"
38 Nightclub routines
40 Evaporate
41 Roof overhangs
47 Come into view
49 Warning sounds
50 Paid out
51 Shopping centers
52 Wild guess
53 Green citrus fruit
54 Notion
55 Jockey's strap
56 Distance unit on a golf course
57 Hammer target
58 Suffix for exist
59 Raison d'___
60 Burglar's booty

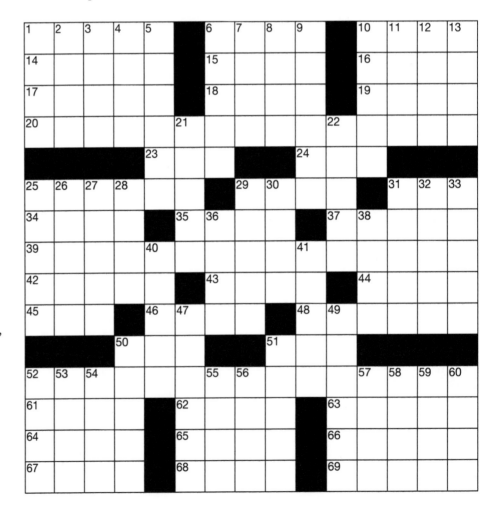

★ Number-Out

Shade squares so that no number appears in any row or column more than once. Shaded squares may not touch each other horizontally or vertically, and all unshaded squares must form a single continuous area.

3	2	3	4	5
2	4	4	4	3
3	5	1	2	4
1	1	1	5	2
4	3	2	3	5

Think Alike

Unscramble the letters in the phrase PEAK EVES to form two words with the same or similar meanings. For example, BEST RATING can be anagrammed to spell START and BEGIN.

_____   _____

Who's What Where?

The correct term for a resident of Thunder Bay, Ontario, is:

A) Thunderer   B) Thunderan

C) Thunder Bayite   D) Thunderbian

★ No Three in a Row

Enter the maze at the top left, pass through all the squares exactly once, then exit, all without retracing your path. You may not pass through three squares of the same color consecutively.

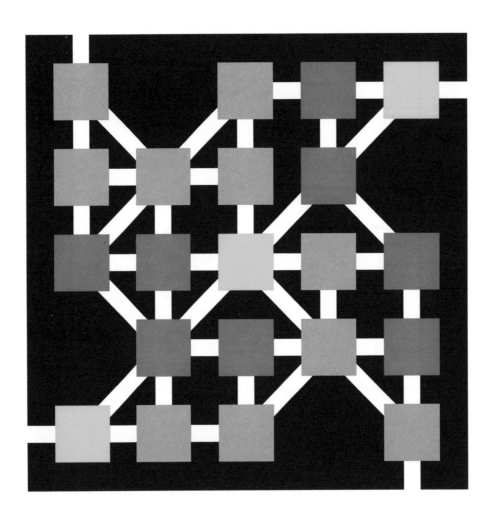

Say It Again

What three-letter word can be either an electrical appliance or a noun meaning "enthusiast"?

___ ___ ___

★ Ellsworth by Gail Grabowski

ACROSS

1 Is concerned
6 Postal delivery
10 Kissing pair
14 Martini garnish
15 Ancient South American
16 Work on, as a manuscript
17 Note from a sweetheart
19 Topnotch
20 Cry of discovery
21 Go out with
22 Lose air, as a tire
24 Parcels out
26 Offer at retail
27 Australian bird
28 Thoroughfares
31 Cry of accomplishment
34 Say the rosary
36 "On the ___ hand ..."
38 Winter vehicles
40 Night bird
41 War horse
42 Braid
43 Have a cry
45 Baseball officials, for short
46 Pestered
48 And so on: Abbr.
50 Graph paper pattern
51 Attack
54 "Here's my phone number"
57 All ___ (attentive)
58 Grassy field
60 Vicinity
61 Mary's nursery rhyme companion

64 Thoughtful
65 Lavish affection (on)
66 City near Phoenix
67 Whirlpool
68 Took to court
69 Got up

DOWN

1 Carbonated drink
2 Waikiki welcome
3 Competitor
4 Night before a holiday
5 Not very often
6 Oven gloves
7 Poker hand starter
8 Frozen water
9 Not as small
10 Salad ingredient
11 Adored celebrity
12 ___ colada
13 Undo a "dele"
18 Completely consume
23 Margarines
25 Female star of a film
26 Fashion
28 Worked on lumber, say
29 Those people
30 Leak slowly
31 Recipe abbreviation
32 "... and to ___ good night!"
33 University official
35 Used oars

37 Map lines: Abbr.
39 Tornado or hurricane
44 Oyster product
47 Lets another car go
49 Sports bar fixtures
51 Despised
52 San Antonio landmark
53 Musical beat
54 Birthday party dessert
55 Desertlike
56 What libraries do
57 Suffix for major
59 Under the covers
62 Debtor's note
63 Give permission to

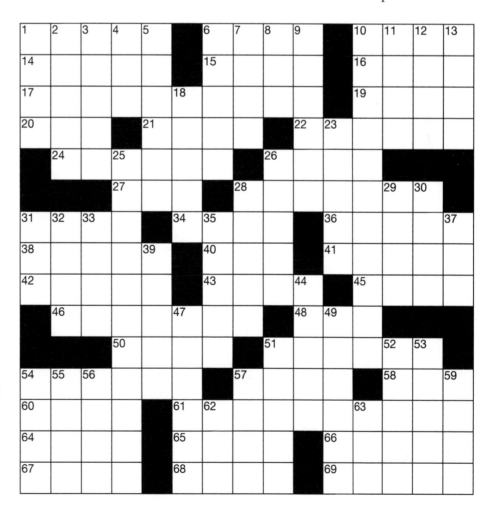

★★ One-Way Streets

The map below represents a set of intersecting streets on which a road rally (starting at A and ending at B) is taking place. The black squares represent checkpoints. You must find a route that starts at A, passes through all checkpoints exactly once, and ends at B. Arrows indicate one-way traffic for that block only. No intersection may be entered more than once.

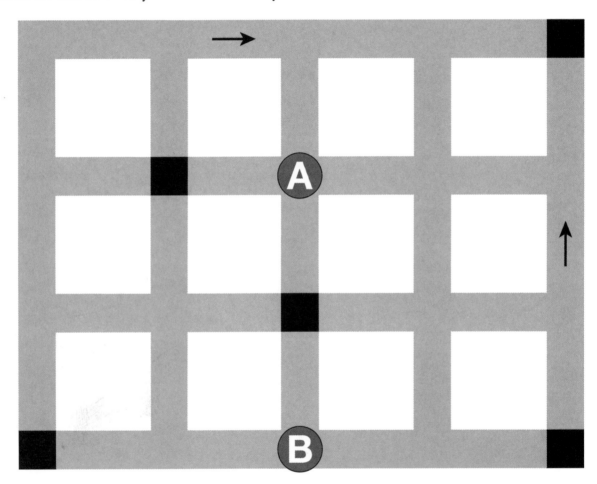

Sound Thinking

The consonant sounds in the word PUFFY are P and F. What six-letter, two-syllable word is pronounced with the same consonant sounds in the same order?

_____

★ Hyper-Sudoku

Fill in the blank squares so that every row, column, 3×3 box, *and* each of the 3×3 gray regions contains the digits 1 through 9 exactly once each.

	9		5		2	3		8
			8	9				1
	2	7	3		1			4
	6			5		4		
	4	8	2					
2		5	4		8			
	1	9		8			3	
					9	1		5
			1		4	8		

C E N T U R Y   M A R K S

Select one number in each of the four columns so that the total adds up to exactly 100.

For example: $\boxed{\frac{6}{8}} + \boxed{\frac{15}{73}} + \boxed{\frac{40}{61}} + \boxed{\frac{29}{37}} = 100$

$$\boxed{\frac{25}{37}} + \boxed{\frac{28}{30}} + \boxed{\frac{26}{40}} + \boxed{\frac{18}{19}} = 100$$

★ Star Search

Can you find the stars hidden in some of the blank squares? Numbered squares indicate how many stars are hidden in the squares adjacent to them in any direction (including diagonally). There is never more than one star in any square.

		1		2		2	
3	3				2	3	
			2			3	
2							2
		2		3	3		
2					2		
	2		2	1			

C H O I C E   W O R D S

Form three six-letter words from the same category by selecting one letter from each column three times. Each letter will be used exactly once.

Example: B A B C O T   Answer: BOBCAT, JAGUAR, OCELOT
          J O E U A R
          O C G L A T

          A R C L E D   _ _ _ _ _ _

          S E I R N E   _ _ _ _ _ _

          V E C A E T   _ _ _ _ _ _

56

★ Discoveries by Gail Grabowski

ACROSS

1 Brazil neighbor
5 Highly seasoned
10 Storage building
14 Sign of the future
15 Pay tribute to
16 Carton sealer
17 Barbecue favorites
18 Alda and Ladd
19 Store sign
20 Discover by research
22 Thick cords
23 Actress Witherspoon
24 Book leaf
25 Gain altitude
28 Sheets and pillowcases
30 Load, as cargo
31 Bee's defense
33 Luau instrument
35 Sandwich meat
36 Afternoon show
38 Play on words
39 Before, in poems
40 Open-mouthed
41 Tadpole's home
42 Oil-carrying ship
44 Word of appreciation
46 Like some dorms
47 Less well-done, as
   steak
49 Army bases
51 Discover by logic
55 Sailor's shout
56 Plumber's concerns
57 Cape Canaveral org.

58 Stand up
59 Major happening
60 Those people
61 Nearly all
62 Campsite shelters
63 Lather

DOWN

1 Cruise stop
2 Middle East ruler
3 Singer McEntire
4 Remove, as a light
   bulb
5 Like a tree-lined
   street
6 Some short-sleeved
   shirts

7 Very impressed
8 State south of Mass.
9 Decade units: Abbr.
10 Underling
11 Discover unexpectedly
12 Fencing weapon
13 Family rooms
21 Barbie's beau
22 Kitchen appliance
24 Cone-bearing tree
25 Tennis great Arthur
26 Begin
27 Discover by chance
28 Part of a poem
29 Polecat
31 Leading actor
32 Waiter's reward

34 Brings to a halt
36 Manufactures
37 Matured
41 Babysitters' employers
43 "Wait a little longer"
44 Has faith in
45 ___ Majesty, the
   Queen
47 Become ready to eat
48 Insurance broker
49 Site for a silo
50 Cleveland's state
51 ___ o'clock shadow
52 Honolulu's island
53 Pre-owned
54 Scottish caps
56 Parakeet or poodle

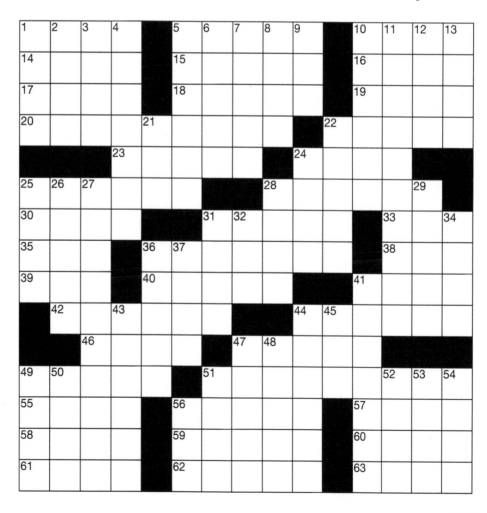

Enter the letters A, B, and C into the diagram, filling in some (but not all) of the squares so that each row and column contains each letter exactly once. The letters outside the diagram indicate the first letter encountered in the indicated row or column when moving in the direction of the arrow from that side of the grid.

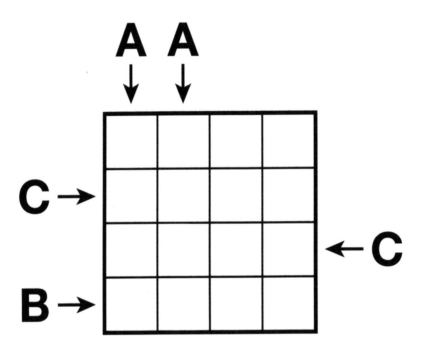

CLUELESS CROSSWORD

Complete the crossword with common, uncapitalized seven-letter words, based on the letters already filled in for you.

	Q		A	R		D
Q	■		■		■	
		Q				E
	■		■	M	■	
R			S	I		S
T	■		■		■	
S	A			I		S

★★ Porcine Pair

Enter the maze from the left as indicated by the arrow, pass through all the stars exactly once each, then exit at right. You may not retrace your path.

Betweener

What three-letter word can go between the two words below so that it forms compound words with both the word preceding it and the word following it?

CROSS __ __ __ BELL

Fill in the blank squares so that every row, column, and 3×3 box contains the digits 1 through 9 exactly once each.

			3	6	8			
9			1	4			7	
5								3
	5		9	6	3			
7								9
			2	7	5		4	
1								8
	3			9	1			7
		4	8	5				

Each line contains a five-letter word and a four-letter word that have been mixed together. (The order of the letters in each word has not been changed.) Unmix the two words on each line and write them in the spaces provided. For example, D A R I U N V E T = DRIVE + AUNT. When you're done, find a two-part answer to the clue by reading down two letter columns in the answers.

CLUE: Choose, in a way

B E D O G I E L D = _ _ _ _ _ + _ _ _ _

H E G R O R W N O = _ _ _ _ _ + _ _ _ _

S A P H O I B E T = _ _ _ _ _ + _ _ _ _

S A W L O R A D S = _ _ _ _ _ + _ _ _ _

★ Dental Work by Sally R. Stein

ACROSS

1 Cushiony
5 Kilt wearer
9 Bert's *Sesame Street* friend
14 Higher than
15 Therefore
16 Intended
17 Numerical information
18 Standard
19 Of the eye
20 Economist Greenspan
21 Craving for sugary foods
23 Winter vehicle
25 "___ the ramparts ..."
26 Wandered around
29 Buddy
31 Big marching band instrument
35 Not qualified
36 Syrup source
38 Fraction of a min.
39 Be scrumptious
42 Sheep sound
43 Brief letters
44 Subside
45 Quantities: Abbr.
47 ___ Aviv
48 Deceived
49 "The Greatest" boxer
51 Young male horse
52 Kid's mouthful
57 Comedy routines
61 Lion sounds
62 Very uncommon
63 Layer of paint
64 Beginning
65 Prayer's last word
66 Past the deadline
67 Dandelions, for example
68 Highest-quality
69 Midterm or final

DOWN

1 Carbonated drink
2 Elliptical shape
3 Greek cheese
4 Send, as a message
5 Felt intuitively
6 Big group of people
7 Mean person
8 Heavy book
9 Ham it up
10 Tell what you've seen
11 U.S. alliance
12 "What's ___ for me?"
13 Engrave deeply
22 Turnpike charges
24 Allow to enter
26 Caribbean dance
27 Midnight follower
28 G sharp equivalent
29 Group of experts
30 Chimps and gorillas
32 Customary
33 Singer Midler
34 Felt sore
36 Tiny speck
37 Computer message
40 Away from home
41 Something in the way
46 Got angry
48 Brief time period
50 Rosters
51 Brings back to health
52 Black bird
53 Sharpen
54 Make simpler
55 Take rudely
56 Polo or parcheesi
58 Persuade
59 "Bye-bye!"
60 Part of a rose

Draw the smallest number of straight lines possible, each from edge to edge, so that at least one line passes through each of the 17 dots.

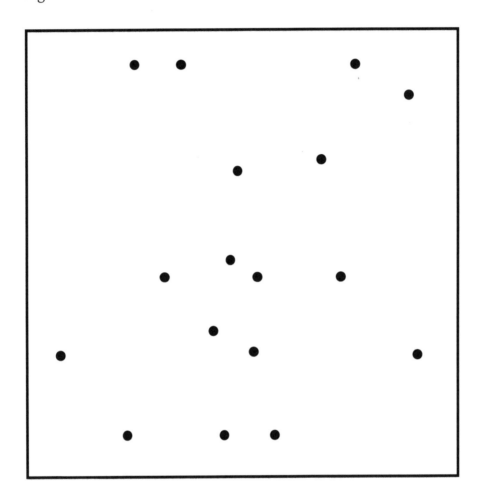

Three of a Kind

Find a set of three hidden words in the sentence that go together in some way. For example, "Chefs were **bus**ily slicing **car**rots and **cab**bage" conceals the set "bus, car, cab."

Don't ask me to choreograph the Banjo Band Ballet.

★★ Find the Ships

Ten ships of four different sizes (shown below left) are hidden in the diagram. Ships may be oriented horizontally or vertically, and may not touch each other, not even diagonally. A square containing wavy lines represents open water; such a square will not contain any part of a ship. Numbers at the edge of the diagram indicate how many squares in that row or column contain parts of ships, including any which may have already been placed as clues.

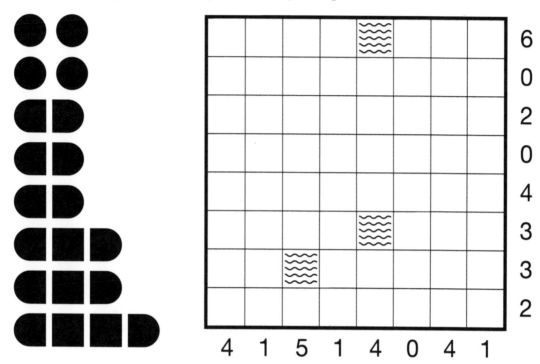

Two-by-Four

The eight letters in the word AUTONOMY can be rearranged in only one way to form a pair of common four-letter words. Can you find them?

— — — —   — — — —

★★ Fences

Connect the dots with vertical or horizontal lines so that a single loop is formed with no crossings or branches. Each number indicates how many lines surround it; squares with no number may be surrounded by any number of lines.

ADDITION SWITCH

Switch the positions of two digits in the incorrect sum at right to get a correct sum. For example, in the incorrect sum 955 + 264 = 411, you would swap the second 1 in 411 with the 9 in 955 to get the correct sum 155 + 264 = 419.

$$237$$
$$+496$$
$$228$$

★ News Items by Gail Grabowski

ACROSS

1 Historical times
5 Discontinues
10 Shoot the breeze
14 Aloe ___
15 Like a gymnast
16 Medal recipient
17 Molecule part
18 Boneless fish
19 Military force
20 Two-film show
23 English class assignment
24 Highways: Abbr.
25 "Man's best friend"
28 U-turn from NNW
29 Fishing pole
32 The land along the coast
34 Jumbled together
36 List entry
37 Upstairs area of a home
41 College cheers
43 Tweety and Sylvester, e.g.
44 Chalkboard correction
48 Small speck
49 Mas' mates
52 Writing instrument
53 Religious group
55 Notify
57 Rabbit's foot, for example
61 Sound in a cave
63 Eagle's claw
64 High-fiber cereal
65 Jump
66 Airplane walkway
67 Change the decor of
68 Hawaiian garlands
69 School transcript entry
70 Citrus drinks

DOWN

1 Gets away from
2 Throw again
3 Stir to action
4 Brazilian ballroom dance
5 Strongbox relative
6 "The weekend's almost here!"
7 Petroleum-carrying ship
8 Fabric folds
9 Small sofa
10 Burn slightly
11 Genetics study
12 Shirt sleeve filler
13 Plaything
21 Song part
22 Nation north of Mex.
26 Poem of praise
27 Diamond or emerald
30 Tic-tac-toe nonwinner
31 Family room
33 Knights' titles
34 Clutter
35 Banned insecticide, briefly
37 China's largest city
38 Lawn material
39 In addition
40 Pub sign
41 Sales agent, briefly
42 "___ you sure?"
45 GI show sponsor
46 Sale merchandise label
47 Cream-filled dessert
49 Looked closely (at)
50 Pinball player's hangout
51 Shorthand pros
54 Oklahoma city
56 Fall zodiac sign
58 Clumsy one's cry
59 Wintry
60 Leg joint
61 Kay follower
62 So-so mark, in school

Fill in the diagram so that each rectangular piece contains the digits 1, 2, and 3 once each, according to these rules: 1) No two horizontally or vertically adjacent squares can contain the same digit. 2) Each completed row and column of the diagram must have an equal number of 1's, 2's, and 3's.

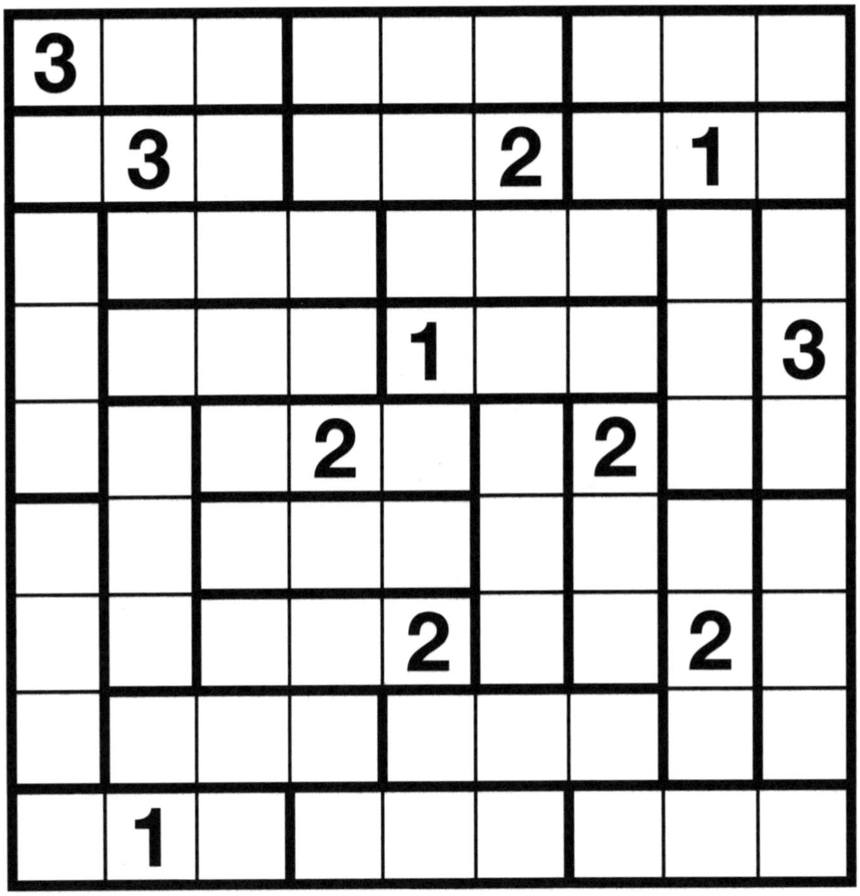

Wrong Is Right

Which of these four words is misspelled?

A) spattula

B) spangle

C) sparsely

D) spatial

Shade squares so that no number appears in any row or column more than once. Shaded squares may not touch each other horizontally or vertically, and all unshaded squares must form a single continuous area.

3	1	4	2	2
4	1	5	3	3
5	1	2	3	4
4	2	1	3	5
2	4	3	1	2

In Other Words

There is only one common uncapitalized word that contains the consecutive sequence of letters WEV. What is the word?

_____

Think Alike

Unscramble the letters in the phrase CITY SHOP to form two words with the same or similar meanings. For example, BEST RATING can be anagrammed to spell START and BEGIN.

_____   _____

ACROSS

1 Doily material
5 Londoner's farewell
9 Dry as a desert
13 Attach, as a shirt button
14 Prepared ground for planting
15 Cornbread
16 Wasn't fooled by fakery
19 In that case
20 "So be it!"
21 Family vehicles
22 Singer McEntire
24 Transgressions
26 Make a change to
29 Loses traction
31 Grade-schooler's transportation
34 Special treat
36 Butterfly-catching device
37 Vatican leader
38 Trying to increase one's salary
41 High-schooler, usually
42 Obtained
43 Old Faithful, for example
44 Suffix for west
45 Jockey's mount
47 Food plans
48 Snake's tooth
49 Roaring feline
51 ___ con carne
54 Significant times
56 Pesky insect
60 Rejoin a group
63 Smell ___ (be suspicious)
64 Stack
65 Dog treats
66 Lawn burrower
67 Driving directions listings: Abbr.
68 Warner ___ (film studio)

DOWN

1 Book page
2 Hole-punching tools
3 Completed, as a comic strip drawing
4 Dir. opposite WSW
5 Inventor Edison
6 First-rate
7 Comparatively small
8 "Classified" listings
9 Very high grade
10 Overwhelming victory
11 Data, for short
12 Dict. entries
13 Biol. or chem.
17 Pat gently
18 Makes illegal
23 Ireland alias
25 Delegate's badge
26 Playing marble
27 Last place finisher
28 Small souvenir
30 Ship's speed units
31 Idaho's capital
32 Topple
33 Fortunetellers
35 Incite
37 Buying, as at a restaurant
39 "No way!"
40 Fix up
45 Mustache material
46 Makes happy
48 Wind instrument
50 Suffix meaning "sort of"
51 Study hard
52 Courageous one
53 Type like *this*: Abbr.
55 Acting job
57 Taboo thing
58 Beerlike beverages
59 Six-pt. football plays
61 *Car Talk* network
62 Abate

★★ Sequence Maze

Enter the maze, pass through all the colored squares exactly once each, then exit, all without retracing your path, with the following condition: you must pass through the colored squares in this sequence: red, blue, yellow, red, blue, yellow, etc. (The correct entrance and exit are for you to determine.)

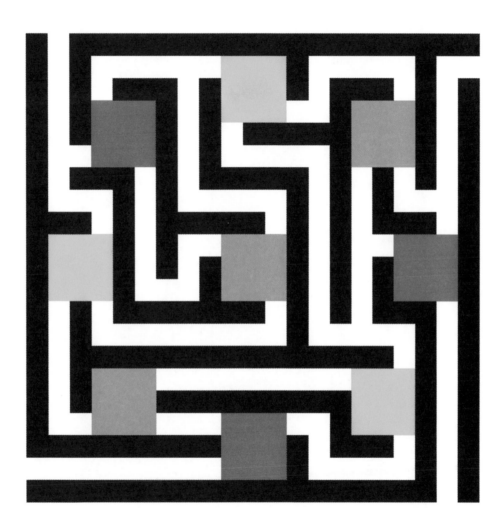

Say It Again

What three-letter word can be either a head movement or a verb meaning "doze"?

—— —— ——

In this crossword puzzle with no clues, each answer consists of two words whose spellings are the same except for the pairs of consecutive letters given. All answers are common words (no phrases), and none are hyphenated or capitalized. Some individual clues may have more than one solution, but only one word pair will correctly link up with all other word pairs.

Transdeletion

Delete one letter from the word BLOTTER and anagram the rest to get something that might hold water.

_____

Fill in the blank squares so that every row, column, 3×3 box, *and* each of the 3×3 gray regions contains the digits 1 through 9 exactly once each.

5	7		8					2
8	3				4	7		6
		9				3		1
							2	5
6				5		7		
3		5	7					
	6		9	5	7			
7				1			9	4
	5	3		8		6	1	

M I X A G R A M S

Each line contains a five-letter word and a four-letter word that have been mixed together. (The order of the letters in each word has not been changed.) Unmix the two words on each line and write them in the spaces provided. For example, D A R I U N V E T = DRIVE + AUNT. When you're done, find a two-part answer to the clue by reading down two letter columns in the answers.

CLUE: Goalie wear

L O C O H A M F E = _ _ _ _ _ + _ _ _ _

S A P U L A M A D = _ _ _ _ _ + _ _ _ _

P L I E S E S C E = _ _ _ _ _ + _ _ _ _

S O A P A C K E R = _ _ _ _ _ + _ _ _ _

★ Sticky Stuff by Gail Grabowski

ACROSS

1 Swiss peaks
5 Milky gems
10 Casual talk
14 Ark builder
15 Granter of wishes
16 Boxcar rider
17 Stereo accessory
19 Once again
20 Not as big
21 Parking lot attendants
23 Paving material
24 Deceptive
26 Poplar trees
29 ___ and rave
30 Train alternative
33 Intelligent
34 Croons a tune
35 Numero ___
36 Is the owner of
37 Likely
38 Zero
39 New Hampshire hrs.
40 Eskimo house
42 Arizona plants
44 That girl
45 College girl
46 Soaked in a tub
47 Produces flowers
49 Everyone
50 In the vicinity
52 Maui and Oahu
56 Phobia
57 Impromptu jazz performance

60 Hard to find
61 Woodwind instruments
62 Singer Fitzgerald
63 Racetrack postings
64 Attack from all sides
65 Ooze slowly

DOWN

1 Household pests
2 Rich soil
3 One of the Three Bears
4 Bus stop structure
5 Rude starers
6 Bosc or Bartlett
7 "___ questions?"
8 Be untruthful
9 Single portion of food
10 Blackboard eraser target
11 Term of endearment
12 Assist a criminal
13 Hauls, as a trailer
18 Shrub or bush
22 Performs in a play
24 Camera stands
25 Moved quickly toward
26 Fireplace remnants
27 Break into pieces
28 Paper towel tube material
31 Join forces
32 Well-built

34 Oregon's capital
40 Computer image
41 Encouraging words to a worker
42 Uses the phone
43 Books with maps
46 Most meanspirited
48 Fishing aids
50 Frizzy hairdo
51 Sit down with a book
52 Words of understanding
53 Cairo's river
54 Ration (out)
55 Ginger cookie
58 "Honest" president
59 May and June: Abbr.

The map below represents a set of intersecting streets on which a road rally is taking place. The black squares represent checkpoints. The S's stand for "start" and "stop," but which is which is left for you to determine. You must find a route that starts at one S, passes through all checkpoints exactly once, and ends at the other S. Arrows indicate one-way traffic for that block only. No intersection may be entered more than once.

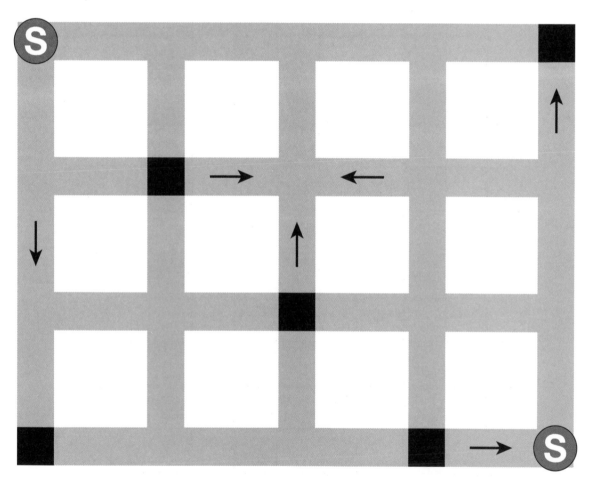

Sound Thinking

Common words whose consonant sounds are R, J, and N (once each, in that order) include REGION and REJOIN. What other six-letter word starting with a different letter is pronounced with the same consonant sounds in the same order?

_____

★★ Tanks a Lot

Enter the maze somewhere at the bottom, pass over all tanks from behind (thereby destroying them), then exit. You may not pass through any square more than once, and may not enter a square in the line of fire of a tank you have not yet destroyed.

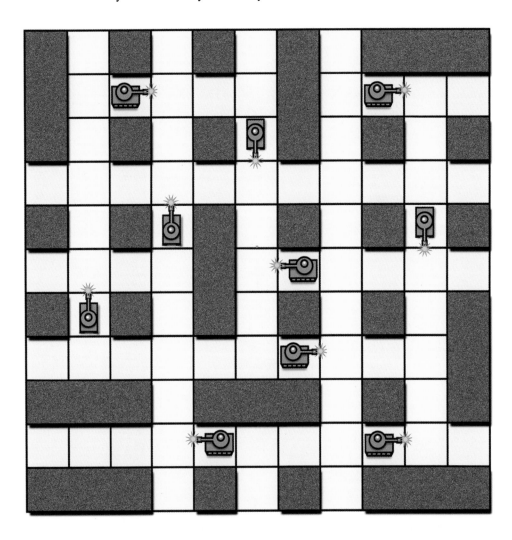

Small Change

Change one letter in each of these two words to form a common two-word phrase. For example, PANTRY CHEW becomes PASTRY CHEF.

YOLK SONS

ACROSS

1 Mama's mate
5 1650, in Roman numerals
9 Swampland
14 Imitative one
15 Cleveland's lake
16 Maui greeting
17 Two "G" nations
20 Praise highly
21 Musical postscript
22 Corp. bigwigs
23 Make angry
25 *Mona* ___
27 Agile
30 Nest egg letters
32 Leapt suddenly
36 Road service org.
37 Sports stadium
39 Speak
40 Two "G" nations
43 So all can hear
44 Actress Lindsay
45 Eisenhower nickname
46 Carpentry machine
48 So far
49 Part of MIT: Abbr.
50 "That makes sense"
52 Apartment payment
54 Can't stand
57 Wheel bar
59 Stage performer
63 Two "G" nations
66 Instruct
67 Canine pests

68 Manager, for short
69 Flower holders
70 Maple or mahogany
71 Platter shape

DOWN

1 Signal via beeper
2 Top of a mountain
3 Impudent
4 National Guard building
5 Guys
6 Popular breakfast food
7 Farewell in Florence
8 Tennis pro Ivan
9 Newsstand buy
10 Separately, on menus
11 After-shower wear
12 "Scram!"
13 Author ___ Christian Andersen
18 ___ Baba
19 Banquet stage
24 Former Italian money
26 Reject scornfully
27 Heroic tales
28 Pop singer Abdul
29 Synthetic fabric
31 Pester
33 Had leftovers, perhaps
34 Narrow parts of bottles
35 Say hello to
37 Chilean mountains

38 Sticking ability
41 Applauding group
42 Fence opening
47 Peruse
49 Wanted to scratch
51 Praise highly
53 Remind persistently
54 *Curb Appeal* cable network
55 Neighborhood
56 Pekoe and oolong
58 Secluded habitat
60 Cabbie's car
61 Change for $5
62 Spice bottle holder
64 Sounds of delight
65 Poor grade

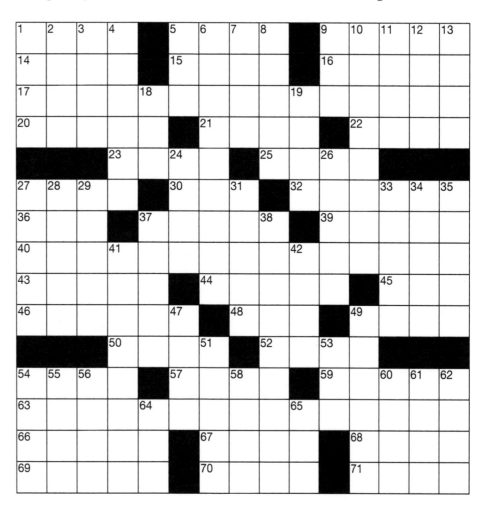

Can you find the stars hidden in some of the blank squares? Numbered squares indicate how many stars are hidden in the squares adjacent to them in any direction (including diagonally). There is never more than one star in any square.

	3		6		1	1	
				2		2	
1			3			2	
	2		2		2		
	3				3	3	
	3	3		1			
					3		
		1		2			

CHOICE WORDS

Form three six-letter words from the same category by selecting one letter from each column three times. Each letter will be used exactly once.

Example: B A B C O T   Answer: BOBCAT, JAGUAR, OCELOT
          J O E U A R
          O C G L A T

          B E D L R T   _ _ _ _ _ _

          F O L M E A   _ _ _ _ _ _

          H E W O E R   _ _ _ _ _ _

★★ Triad Split Decisions

In this crossword puzzle with no clues, each answer consists of two words whose spellings are the same except for the sets of three consecutive letters given. All answers are common words (no phrases), and none are hyphenated or capitalized. Some individual clues may have more than one solution, but only one word pair will correctly link up with all other word pairs.

Transdeletion

Delete one letter from the word UNTIMED and anagram the rest to get another word associated with time.

_____

ACROSS

1 Four Corners state
5 Realty listings
10 Auction offers
14 Ibsen heroine
15 Goolagong rival
16 Singer Adams
17 Colorado mountains
19 What there "oughta be"
20 Belief system
21 Conduct, as a meeting
22 Sheets of plywood
24 Sycophants
26 Juicy pear
27 Current regime
28 Gas-saving arrangements
32 Pile up
35 *Kon-___*
36 Russian river
37 Chicken wire
38 French impressionist painter
39 Emperor before Galba
40 Slightest trace
41 Thunderstruck
42 Tend, as a fire
43 Takes to the cleaners
45 Ginnie ___
46 Split apart
47 Make rainbows
51 Not high-quality
54 Unchanged
55 Yonder damsel
56 Antler
57 Success/failure phrase

60 Poet's black
61 More slippery, probably
62 Sloping walk
63 Civil rights leader Parks
64 Singing cowboy
65 Wallet fillers

DOWN

1 Not suitable
2 Sculptor's rendering
3 Olfactory stimulus
4 Harrison, in *Star Wars*
5 Medal recipients
6 Face shapes
7 Heal, as a bone

8 Unit of work
9 "Hurry!"
10 Obsessive quantifier
11 Not moving
12 Station changer
13 Hems or bastes
18 Adds turpentine to
23 Cobra cousin
25 Cable alternative
26 Sweltered
28 They may climb the walls
29 Layered cookie
30 Carefree escapade
31 Gin fizz flavor
32 Left Bank chums
33 Catty remark

34 Italian wine city
35 Castle part
38 Kuala Lumpur locale
42 More secure
44 ___ Moines, Iowa
45 Part of ROM
47 Croupier, often
48 Lake Nasser city
49 Doorbell sound
50 Short-term workers
51 *Moonstruck* Oscar winner
52 Freight hopper
53 Piccadilly statue
54 Tizzy
58 Hosp. area
59 Sign of a sellout

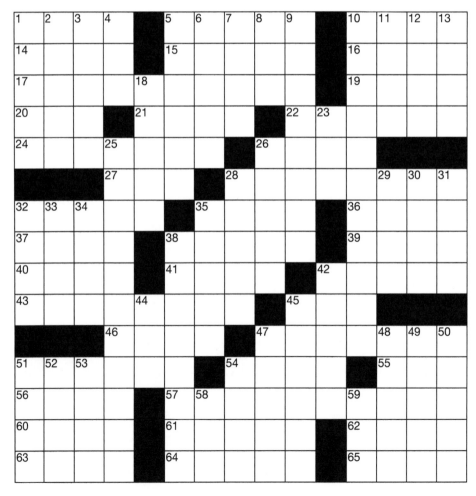

Enter the letters A, B, and C into the diagram, filling in some (but not all) of the squares so that each row and column contains each letter exactly once. The letters outside the diagram indicate the first letter encountered in the indicated row or column when moving in the direction of the arrow from that side of the grid.

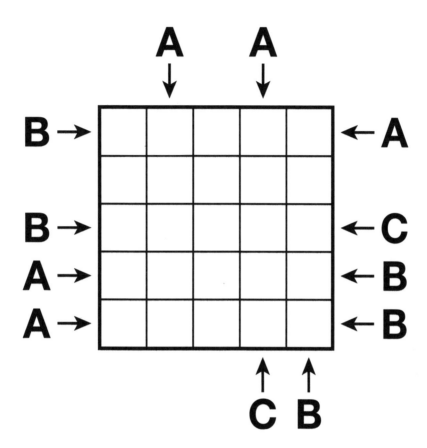

National Treasure

There is one common six-letter word that can be formed from the letters in ALBANIAN. What is it?

— — — — — —

★★ Find the Ships

Ten ships of four different sizes (shown below left) are hidden in the diagram. Ships may be oriented horizontally or vertically, and may not touch each other, not even diagonally. A square containing wavy lines represents open water; such a square will not contain any part of a ship. Numbers at the edge of the diagram indicate how many squares in that row or column contain parts of ships, including any which may have already been placed as clues.

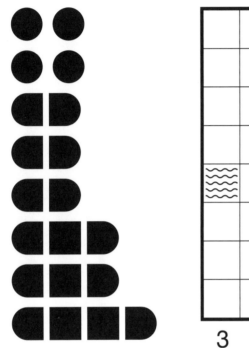

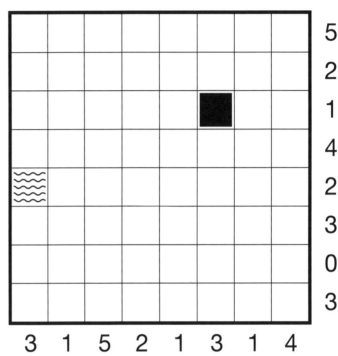

Two-by-Four

The eight letters in the word BALLYHOO can be rearranged in three different ways to form a pair of common four-letter words. Can you find all three pairs?

___ ___ ___ ___   ___ ___ ___ ___

___ ___ ___ ___   ___ ___ ___ ___

___ ___ ___ ___   ___ ___ ___ ___

★★ Plane Speaking by Fred Piscop

ACROSS

1 Bit of china
6 Nobelist Wiesel
10 Cambridge sch.
13 Hairstyling shop
14 Dickens's "little" girl
15 Tibetan priest
16 Glibness
18 Memorable times
19 More minute
20 Wild one
22 Secret meeting
25 Talk out of
26 Club fund-raiser
30 Completely wreck
32 Banish
33 "Toodle-oo!"
34 Folk singer Joan
38 *Born Free* lioness
39 Desert dearth
40 Jazzy Fitzgerald
41 Riga resident
42 Numbered work
43 Like most people
44 Shady spot
46 Courage
47 Congo's onetime name
50 Direct elsewhere
52 Pay no heed to
54 Really steamed
59 Flamingo color
60 All settled up
63 Ballet bend
64 Actress Taylor
65 Make fixes to
66 "Indeed!"
67 Dinner veggies
68 Paddock papas

DOWN

1 Furtive "Hey, you!"
2 Poor, as excuses go
3 Natural soother
4 Cel character
5 Grant the right (to)
6 Diary note
7 Grazing spot
8 Under the weather
9 Fraternal fellows
10 French Revolution figure
11 Mental picture
12 Stun gun
15 100% effort
17 "Take this, please"
21 Tooth care org.
23 Body height
24 Mall bags
26 Film spool
27 Wheel holder
28 Pug's weapon
29 Without a cent
31 Paving goo
33 Come to a point
35 Stepped down
36 Airline to Ben-Gurion
37 Novelist Grey
39 "That's really something!"
43 Puts fizz into
45 Anthem contraction
46 Department store department
47 Full of energy
48 Mentally quick
49 CORE leader
51 Artist's "Done!"
53 Hard to grasp
55 Notes after do
56 State confidently
57 Heredity unit
58 Some linemen
61 Route word
62 Shade provider

★★ Two Pairs

Among the 16 pictures below, find the two pairs of pictures that are identical to each other.

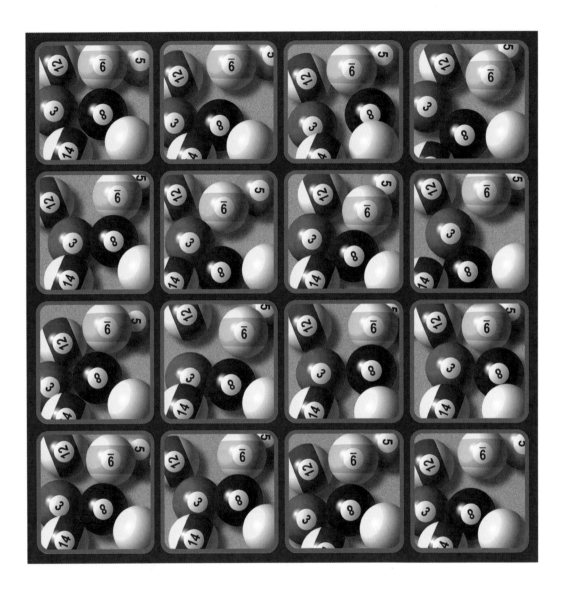

Betweener

What four-letter word can go between the two words below so that it forms compound words with both the word preceding it and the word following it?

TRAP ___ ___ ___ ___ **MAT**

Fill in the blank squares so that every row, column, and 3×3 box contains the digits 1 through 9 exactly once each.

7							1	
	8			5				
		6		1	7	2	3	
9				7				
6	4		3	1	9		7	8
			5					4
1	2	3	4		6			
			8			6		
	5							2

M I X A G R A M S

Each line contains a five-letter word and a four-letter word that have been mixed together. (The order of the letters in each word has not been changed.) Unmix the two words on each line and write them in the spaces provided. For example, D A R I U N V E T = DRIVE + AUNT. When you're done, find a two-part answer to the clue by reading down two letter columns in the answers.

CLUE: Fancy footwear

V I T H E W U S S = _ _ _ _ _ + _ _ _ _

B I R A S I O N S = _ _ _ _ _ + _ _ _ _

P A L O R I N G E = _ _ _ _ _ + _ _ _ _

R O S U P G A T E = _ _ _ _ _ + _ _ _ _

Connect the dots with vertical or horizontal lines so that a single loop is formed with no crossings or branches. Each number indicates how many lines surround it; squares with no number may be surrounded by any number of lines.

```
 3     3     0  1  2

 3

    1  1                3

                        0  2

 3  0

    2           3  3

                           1

    2  1  3     1     3
```

Wrong Is Right

Which of these four words is misspelled?

A) autumnal   B) auspicious

C) auxilary   D) auteur

★★ Fowl Language by Daniel R. Stark

ACROSS

1 Pirate's booty
5 Unpleasant situation
9 Manufacturer
14 The good guy
15 Operatic piece
16 Video game pioneer
17 Sandwich cookie
18 Ragtime dance
20 Thick fog
22 Whim
23 Space station view
25 ___ voyage party
26 Stick (to)
29 Breakfast orders
33 Military cells
34 Forest clearing
35 Taunting laugh
37 Loud sound
38 Ancient Britons
39 Be bold
40 Come to the rescue of
41 Sheep shelters
42 Forward thrust
43 Like some power
45 Poked fun at
46 Ben-___
47 Chimney nester
49 With suspicion

53 Ships' steering devices
57 Get too scared
59 Vaccine type
60 Church contribution
61 Foot part
62 Telegraph
63 Campaign tactic
64 Poor grades
65 Scholarship basis

DOWN

1 Bargain-hunt
2 Used to be
3 Environs
4 Zero, in sports slang
5 Ripe
6 Spew lava
7 Polite word
8 Munro's pen name
9 Spring fest need
10 Bring into accord
11 Malden of *Patton*
12 Cupid alias
13 Religious ceremony
19 Implants
21 Rowing implements
24 Screams
26 "Dancing Queen" band
27 Flow out
28 Krishna worshiper
30 Gymnasts' pads
31 Be gracious
32 An NCO, informally

34 "___ move on!"
36 Pay attention to
38 Strong-arm
39 Crouch
41 Old jalopy
42 Feudal boss
44 Latin dance
45 Ends of rivers
48 Temporary peace
49 Behaves
50 Furniture leg leveler
51 Tailed toy
52 Oklahoma city
54 Toledo's lake
55 Like blue moons
56 Malamute's burden
58 Small bill

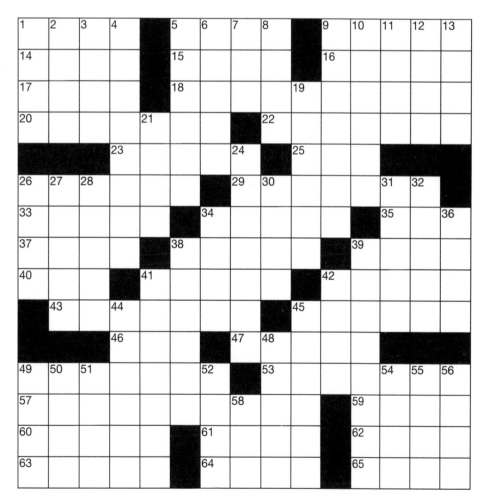

Shade squares so that no number appears in any row or column more than once. Shaded squares may not touch each other horizontally or vertically, and all unshaded squares must form a single continuous area.

4	5	6	1	2	6
2	1	5	4	3	4
3	1	3	4	2	2
3	6	2	4	5	1
3	4	2	6	3	3
6	3	4	5	1	1

Initial Reaction

Identify the well-known proverb from the first letters of each of its words. For example: L. B. Y. L. = Look before you leap.

A. N. B. S. C. _____

Think Alike

Unscramble the letters in the phrase EXTRA COB to form two words with the same or similar meanings. For example, BEST RATING can be anagrammed to spell START and BEGIN.

_____   _____

★★ Hyper-Sudoku

Fill in the blank squares so that every row, column, 3×3 box, *and* each of the 3×3 gray regions contains the digits 1 through 9 exactly once each.

		4						7
					9			
7						2		
3				9				
				1	5		8	4
		8					5	6
1					3		2	
8		3	5	2		4		9
2					4	7		

C E N T U R Y   M A R K S

Select one number in each of the four columns so that the total adds up to exactly 100.

For example:

$$\boxed{\frac{6}{\underline{8}}} + \boxed{\frac{\overline{15}}{73}} + \boxed{\frac{\overline{40}}{61}} + \boxed{\frac{29}{\underline{37}}} = 100$$

$$\boxed{\frac{26}{8}} + \boxed{\frac{11}{20}} + \boxed{\frac{60}{18}} + \boxed{\frac{12}{15}} = 100$$

★★ On Your Feet by Fred Piscop

ACROSS

1 Footnote abbr.
6 Stately trees
10 5K or marathon
14 Carried
15 Honest-to-goodness
16 McGregor of *Star Wars* films
17 Glassy look
18 "Render ___ Caesar ..."
19 Wheeled convenience
20 Overcome cold feet
23 Ballpark fig.
24 Less usual
25 Get ripe
29 Toil away
32 Brewpub selections
33 Socially smooth
34 Comics bark
37 Olmos movie of 1987
41 Pig stealer of rhyme
42 Spring up
43 Zero
44 Like marzipan
45 Gave no stars to
47 Wheat or rice
50 Is able to
51 Make it big
57 Film with a cast of thousands
58 Ball game delayer
59 Flags down
62 Part of UPC
63 Like fine wine
64 Riverbank cavorter
65 Small bills
66 ___ a soul
67 Puts an edge on

DOWN

1 Outmoded: Abbr.
2 Place for bets
3 Rugged rock
4 Concerning, in a memo
5 Move unsteadily
6 Blow one's top
7 Easter ends it
8 SAT component
9 Tart fruit
10 Fall back
11 Oscar or Emmy
12 Work on the turkey
13 Sign up
21 "___ no hooks"
22 Ludlum work
25 Sail support
26 Choir member
27 Bulls or Bears
28 SEAL's org.
29 Like a bubble bath
30 Weigh down
31 St. crosser
33 Foul mood
34 Mary Kay competitor
35 Actress Russo
36 Wilma's toon mate
38 Discourage
39 Verb with thou
40 Rustic stopover
44 Siblings' daughters
45 Hole number
46 "You bet!"
47 ___-Roman wrestling
48 Wisconsin college town
49 Out of the way
50 Halloween haul
52 Algerian port
53 Long story
54 Stadium feature
55 Swearing-in words
56 Tiny amount
60 ___ be (don't bother)
61 AARP members: Abbr.

Group all the symbols into sets of three, with each set having either all the same shape in three different colors, or three different shapes of the same color. The symbols in each set must all be connected to each other by common horizontal or vertical sides.

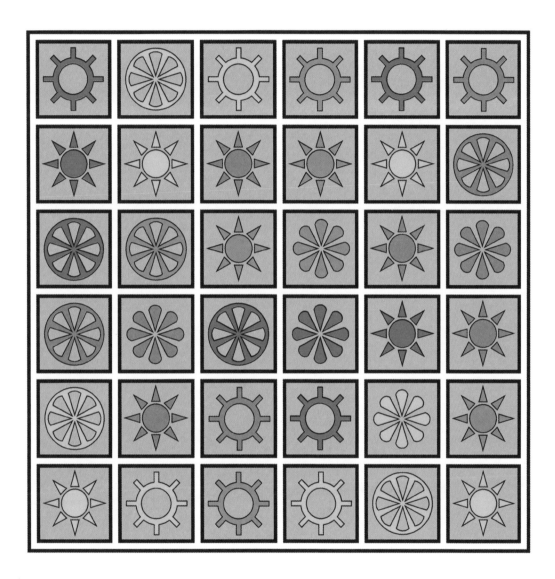

Say It Again

What four-letter word can be either a piece of land or a verb meaning "scheme"?

— — — —

★★ One-Way Streets

The map below represents a set of intersecting streets on which a road rally is taking place. The black squares represent checkpoints. The S's stand for "start" and "stop," but which is which is left for you to determine. You must find a route that starts at one S, passes through all checkpoints exactly once, and ends at the other S. Arrows indicate one-way traffic for that block only. No intersection may be entered more than once.

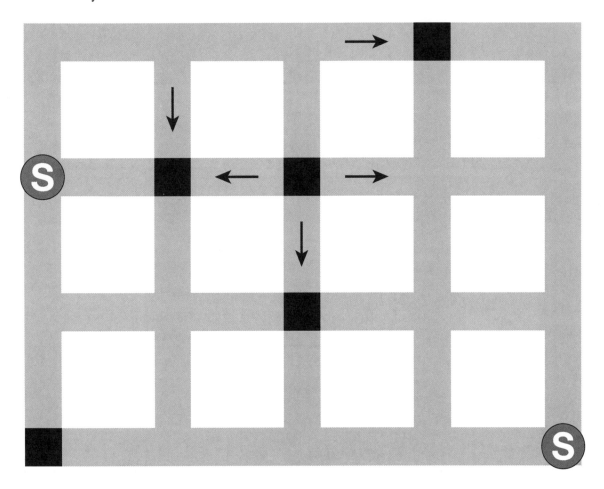

Sound Thinking

The consonant sounds in the word ICEFALL are S, F, and L. What more common seven-letter word is pronounced with the same consonant sounds in the same order?

_____

★★ Wrecking Crew by Kevin Donovan

ACROSS

1 Grist producers
6 Minty drink
11 Shakespearean prince
14 Ta-ta, in Toulon
15 Japanese port
16 Tokyo's former name
17 Cryptologist, often
19 "I figured it out!"
20 *The Right Stuff* author
21 Fortuneteller's card
23 Speak sharply to
27 Tattletale
28 Unexpected guest
32 Thought products
33 Get into
34 Society gal
37 Counter's intervals
38 Some insect encounters
39 Written reminder
40 Particular period
41 Prepared for a long fight
42 Neighbor separator
43 Rodeo entrant
45 Fish hawk
48 Wipes out
49 Utter confusion
50 Bee-like
53 Metal in pewter
54 Kind of crook
60 Gridiron position
61 Happify
62 Set for special occasions
63 Brighton brew
64 Takes a chance
65 Gone from one's plate

DOWN

1 PC alternative
2 Oath affirmation
3 Pot top
4 Washington and ___ University
5 Underground trains
6 "Piano Man" artist
7 High-flying org.
8 Place for a dip
9 Barely earn, with "out"
10 Starsky, to Hutch
11 One of 13 cards
12 Kind of committee
13 Not eager
18 Program for a future lt.
22 It's all around
23 Malicious feeling
24 Two-time Green Party candidate
25 Trade show site
26 Sch. auxiliaries
27 ___ *Gotta Have It* (1986 film)
29 Time at the top
30 Comic caper
31 Shorthand expert
34 Meteor marks
35 Introduction maker
36 Certain South Africans
38 Hazard marker
39 Arizona city
41 Got ready to go out
42 Heat producer
43 Sis's sib
44 Pessimistic investor
45 Santa's reindeer, for example
46 Polish up
47 Black-and-white herbivore
50 At a great distance
51 Sampras of tennis
52 Finishes, as a cake
55 ___ carte
56 Half a dance name
57 Caboodle complement
58 Compass pt.
59 Sought a seat

Fill in the diagram so that each rectangular piece contains the digits 1, 2, and 3 once each, according to these rules: 1) No two horizontally or vertically adjacent squares can contain the same digit.
2) Each completed row and column of the diagram must have an equal number of 1's, 2's, and 3's.

Three of a Kind

Find a set of three hidden words in the sentence that go together in some way. For example, "Chefs were **bus**ily slicing **car**rots and **cab**bage" conceals the set "bus, car, cab."

The nickel-plated garden tool is used for weeding.

★★ Line Drawing

Draw six straight lines from edge to edge so that each line passes through exactly four letters that spell a common word reading from one end of the line to the other (not necessarily left-to-right or top-to-bottom).

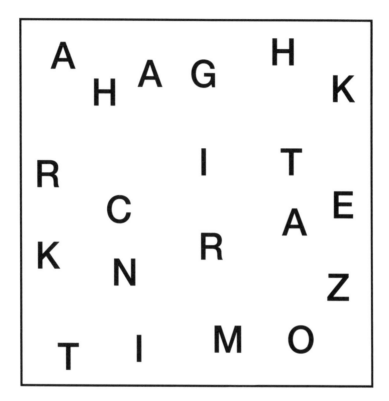

S U D O K U S U M

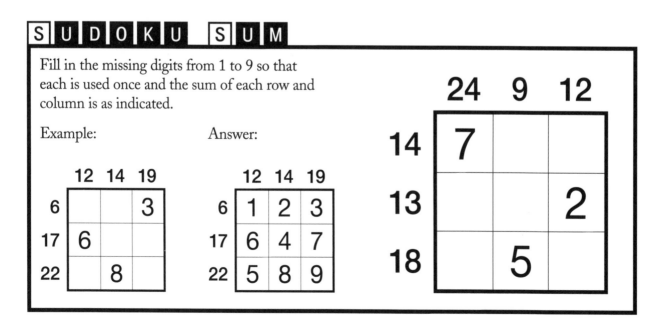

Fill in the missing digits from 1 to 9 so that each is used once and the sum of each row and column is as indicated.

Example:

	12	14	19
6			3
17	6		
22		8	

Answer:

	12	14	19
6	1	2	3
17	6	4	7
22	5	8	9

	24	9	12
14	7		
13			2
18		5	

★★ Triple Treat by Fred Piscop

ACROSS

1 Drew back
6 Pundit's column
10 Mosque leader
14 Marquee posting
15 Scarlett's home
16 Eat well
17 Banquet wear
19 Emporium sign abbr.
20 College term
21 Wipes clean
23 Musical talent
24 Bill of fashion
25 *Casablanca* star
29 Small cut
30 P.D. alert
33 Sailboat pole
34 Mason's material
35 "Roth" plan
36 Slanted: Abbr.
37 Backbone
38 Composer Stravinsky
39 Knock, in the 'hood
40 Tempted
41 Lodge member
42 USNA grad
43 Gets mellower
44 Commandment breaker
45 Burn a bit
47 Sharpshooter's skill
48 Power failure
50 Names to a job
55 Pretense
56 Beef entrée
58 San ___ Obispo, California
59 Trident prong
60 Finely honed
61 "This can't be!"
62 Gets firm
63 Render unreadable

DOWN

1 Norms: Abbr.
2 Bring on board
3 Tabloids twosome
4 Choice word
5 Sweet course
6 Catchall category
7 Ark unit
8 Go astray
9 Article lead-in
10 Think tank nuggets
11 Musical set in Vietnam
12 Chip in
13 Prescriptions, for short
18 "Hurry!" to an MD
22 Assign stars to
24 Fair-haired one
25 Back of a hit single
26 Agree to take part
27 Laundry challenge
28 Feel bad
29 Messy pads
31 Plain talk
32 Less adorned
34 Mall binge
37 Insinuates
38 Charged atom
40 Singer k.d.
41 Brunch libations
44 Uses a snifter
46 Playground retort
47 Church recesses
48 Scandinavian capital
49 Informal refusal
50 "If it ___ broke ..."
51 Allergy symptom
52 Word form for "nerve"
53 London art gallery
54 Depot posting, for short
57 Michelle of the LPGA

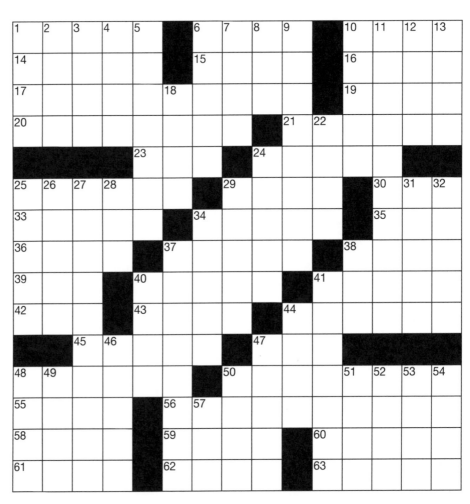

Can you find the stars hidden in some of the blank squares? Numbered squares indicate how many stars are hidden in the squares adjacent to them in any direction (including diagonally). There is never more than one star in any square.

		2			
		5		1	
	2				2
			3	2	
	4		2		
	3				
	3		1		
2			3		
			3	1	

CHOICE WORDS

Form three six-letter words from the same category by selecting one letter from each column three times. Each letter will be used exactly once.

Example: B A B C O T   Answer: BOBCAT, JAGUAR, OCELOT
          J O E U A R
          O C G L A T

A A A C J E   _ _ _ _ _ _

N P V U T E   _ _ _ _ _ _

P A I A H O   _ _ _ _ _ _

Group the dice into sets of two or more whose sums equal nine. The dice in each set must be connected to each other by common horizontal or vertical sides.

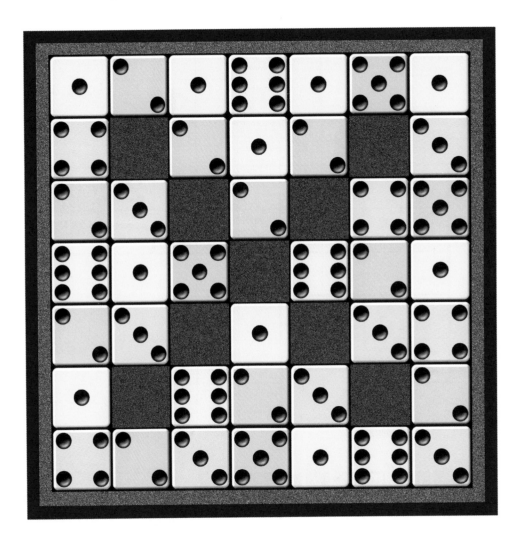

Small Change

Change one letter in each of these two words to form a common two-word phrase. For example, PANTRY CHEW becomes PASTRY CHEF.

HUSK HONEY

_____

★★ Fasten-ation by Fred Piscop

ACROSS

1 Churns up
6 Tourists' aids
10 Mil. unit
13 Reader's download
14 Not to mention
15 ___ Beach, Florida
16 Alley target
18 Optimist's words
19 Neptune's realm
20 Hecklers' chorus
21 Bring forward, as in evidence
23 Hugs, in a letter
24 Took the wheel
25 Nucleus component
29 Slacks fabric
30 Low-calorie
31 Any day now
32 Singer Amos
36 Neutral shade
37 One of a 1492 trio
38 The Bard's river
39 Consider
40 "Woe is me!"
41 Piece of asparagus
42 Industry big shot
44 *Tristram Shandy* author
45 Kvetchers
48 *Norma* ___
49 Jockeying great Eddie
50 Sound of surprise
51 Bat wood
54 French comic actor
55 Medicine chest item
58 Airline to Ben-Gurion
59 Toledo's lake
60 Perrier rival
61 Draft org.
62 Puts on
63 Chars

DOWN

1 Lee's soldiers
2 Double reed
3 Cedar Rapids's state
4 Online guffaw
5 Vail footwear
6 Myopic toon
7 Yodelers' locale
8 Air pump letters
9 Short piano piece
10 Come up again
11 Elegance
12 In great shape
15 TV watcher's cassette
17 Time for lunch, perhaps
22 Cozy room
24 Bar servings
25 Argued in court
26 Paella ingredient
27 Cruel dude
28 Concise, as a sketch
29 Schwarzenegger role
31 Cylindrical structures
33 All done
34 Horse's color
35 Concerning
37 Repeated without understanding
41 Treeless plains
43 ___ Lingus
44 Miss America attire
45 Chess wins
46 Paperless exams
47 Perform the function of
48 Has status
50 Enter
51 Where Siberia is
52 Play the lead
53 Egg layers
56 Precious metal, in Mexico
57 St. crosser

Fill in the blank squares so that every row, column, 3×3 box, *and* each of the 3×3 gray regions contains the digits 1 through 9 exactly once each.

9					5			
1							2	
7		5			1		4	8
6			4	5			7	3
		7			2			
		8					1	5
3		6				9		
							5	
		9			8	7		

M I X A G R A M S

Each line contains a five-letter word and a four-letter word that have been mixed together. (The order of the letters in each word has not been changed.) Unmix the two words on each line and write them in the spaces provided. For example, D A R I U N V E T = DRIVE + AUNT. When you're done, find a two-part answer to the clue by reading down two letter columns in the answers.

CLUE: Scarecrow's accessory?

C H E R R E D O B = _ _ _ _ _ + _ _ _ _

O D A D L I D E Y = _ _ _ _ _ + _ _ _ _

B R O W E V U L E = _ _ _ _ _ + _ _ _ _

N U D E R S B E T = _ _ _ _ _ + _ _ _ _

Enter the letters A, B, and C into the diagram, filling in some (but not all) of the squares so that each row and column contains each letter exactly once. The letters outside the diagram indicate the first letter encountered in the indicated row or column when moving in the direction of the arrow from that side of the grid.

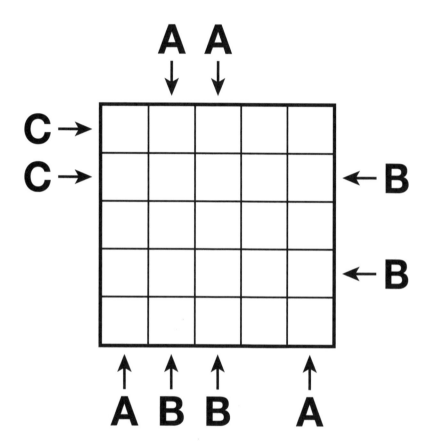

National Treasure

What six-letter world nation can be formed from the letters in URUGUAYAN?

     ___ ___ ___ ___ ___ ___

★★ All Talk by Norma Steinberg

ACROSS

1 Portfolio component
6 Appear to be
10 Jack Horner's find
14 Zoo beast
15 Rod between wheels
16 Ready to harvest
17 Neighborhoods
18 Cash drawer
19 Get ___ (exact revenge)
20 Actress Arthur
21 Mood
24 Designer Calvin
26 Doesn't look forward to
27 Machinery lubricant
29 Sautéed
31 Bank transaction
32 Type of evergreen
34 Traveler in a motorcade
37 Beasts of burden
39 EarthLink alternative
40 Boulder
42 Part of a week
43 Riviera city
46 Potatoes alternative
47 Planted
48 Polar topping
50 Long for
53 Match
54 Checkout choice
57 Yoko ___
60 Horse race distance, perhaps
61 Newspaper piece
62 Sea explorer
64 Actress Lena

65 Put together
66 Perfect
67 Safety devices
68 Epochs
69 Stay awhile

DOWN

1 *Pequod* captain
2 Father
3 Prohibition-era hangout
4 DC water watchdog
5 Throws softly
6 *Paradise Lost* character
7 Way out
8 She, in Chamonix
9 Tuneful
10 Future doc's courses
11 *The Sopranos* mother
12 Overturn
13 Uses tape on
22 Cravats
23 Lets loose
25 Narrow way
27 Happy
28 Santa ___, California
29 Palm branch
30 Precept
33 Window section
34 Film narration work
35 Ancient South American
36 Henhouse sound
38 Cross the goal line
41 Part of a grove
44 "Like, stupendous!"
45 Source of interstate info
47 Vamps
49 Bank offering
50 Evil spirit
51 Napoleon's punishment
52 Leave, so to speak
53 Subordinate staffers
55 Box for practice
56 Mother of Castor and Pollux
58 Close at hand
59 Parisian airport
63 Wyo. neighbor

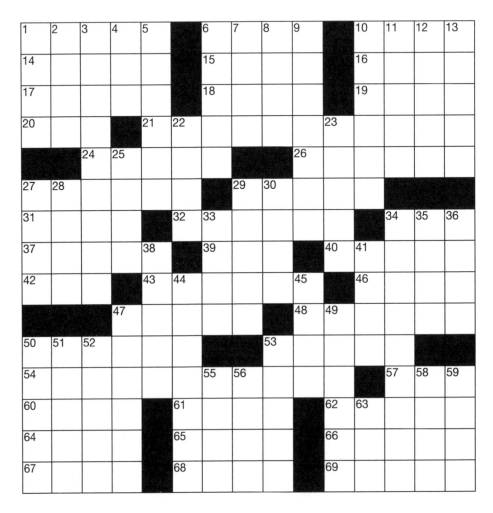

★★ Find the Ships

Ten ships of four different sizes (shown below left) are hidden in the diagram. Ships may be oriented horizontally or vertically, and may not touch each other, not even diagonally. A square containing wavy lines represents open water; such a square will not contain any part of a ship. Numbers at the edge of the diagram indicate how many squares in that row or column contain parts of ships, including any which may have already been placed as clues.

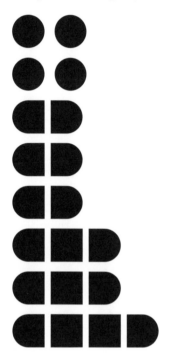

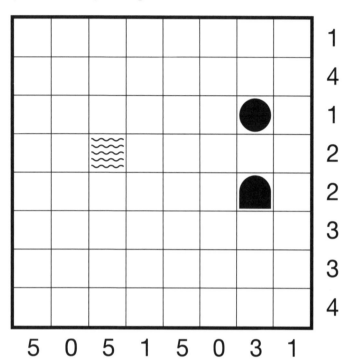

Betweener

What four-letter word can go between the two words below so that it forms compound words with both the word preceding it and the word following it?

KIN __ __ __ __ **LORE**

Two-by-Four

The eight letters in the name COLUMBUS can be rearranged in only one way to form a pair of common four-letter words. Can you find them?

__ __ __ __   __ __ __ __

In this crossword puzzle with no clues, each answer consists of two words whose spellings are the same except for the sets of three consecutive letters given. All answers are common words (no phrases), and none are hyphenated or capitalized. Some individual clues may have more than one solution, but only one word pair will correctly link up with all other word pairs.

Transdeletion

Delete one letter from the word BARGAIN and anagram the rest to get a two-word term for a type of safety device.

ACROSS

1 Prolonged military attack
6 Consider
10 Gullible sorts
14 Former Second Family
15 Inventor's germ
16 Bard's river
17 Small aircraft
20 Level-headed
21 Painting the town, perhaps
22 Tilter's weapon
23 Stage accessory
25 Hire, as a bus
27 African monkey
30 Old buddy
31 *Middlemarch* author
32 Side with a burger
33 DJ's stack
36 Multiple allegiance
40 Typesetting widths
41 Outfielder's call
42 Getting chilled
43 Sturm und ___
45 Like Dolly the sheep
46 Newman once of *SNL*
49 Not very busy
50 Run ___ of the law
51 Poor grade
52 Did the crawl
56 Risk-it-all bet
60 Art Deco master
61 Bikini parts
62 Emphatic denial
63 Feeder filler
64 Actress Neuwirth
65 Freezing temperatures

DOWN

1 Some NCOs
2 Council Bluffs' state
3 March 17 slogan word
4 Hereditary collection
5 Language suffix
6 Unearth
7 Cut and paste
8 Bard's nightfall
9 Daisy ___ (Capp character)
10 Yearly earnings
11 ___-garde
12 Puerto Rican city
13 Villainous look
18 When morning ends
19 Map out
24 Campus military org.
25 It's all the rage
26 "Mr. Hockey"
27 *Adam* ___ (31-Across work)
28 Reunion attendee
29 Skewed view
30 Static annoyance
32 Children's author R.L.
33 Goatee site
34 Monopoly pair
35 Floored it
37 Bowie's model wife
38 Court plea, for short
39 Racket-shaped footwear
43 Painted sloppily
44 Lunar valley
45 Jazz singer Laine
46 Weighs down
47 Ere
48 Letter carrier's beat
49 Have a feeling
51 Not colorful
53 Like Solomon
54 Has ___ (is connected)
55 Dept. bosses
57 Fall back
58 Aluminum source
59 Blaster's need

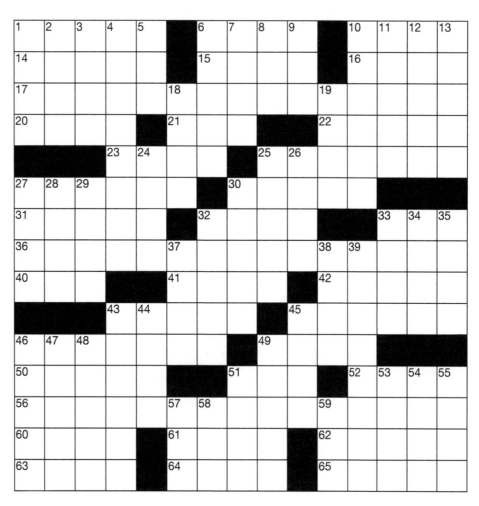

Fill in the diagram so that each rectangular piece contains the digits 1, 2, and 3 once each, according to these rules: 1) No two horizontally or vertically adjacent squares can contain the same digit. 2) Each completed row and column of the diagram must have an equal number of 1's, 2's, and 3's.

Wrong Is Right

Which of these four words is misspelled?

A) obsolescent

B) aquiescent

C) reminiscent

D) munificent

Connect the dots with vertical or horizontal lines so that a single loop is formed with no crossings or branches. Each number indicates how many lines surround it; squares with no number may be surrounded by any number of lines.

ADDITION SWITCH

Switch the positions of two digits in the incorrect sum at right to get a correct sum. For example, in the incorrect sum 955 + 264 = 411, you would swap the second 1 in 411 with the 9 in 955 to get the correct sum 155 + 264 = 419.

$$776$$
$$+808$$
$$814$$

★★ Compromise by Fred Piscop

ACROSS

1 Tennis great Rod
6 Work detail, for short
10 Wild guess
14 Still in the game
15 "No contest," for one
16 Hearty partner
17 Retreat
19 Any of the Joads
20 Rating unit
21 Mag. staffers
22 Dream up
24 Buck or bull
26 Takes to the cleaners
27 Cleopatra's love
30 Hot dog topper
31 Get on the plane
32 Completely wreck
33 Usher's offering
36 Gospel writer
37 ___ acid (B vitamin)
38 Say grace, say
39 Compass reading: Abbr.
40 Like dried mud
41 Access AOL
42 Chance happenings
44 Jennifer Lopez role
45 Wiggly dessert
47 Potting need
48 Gotten up
49 Green prefix

50 Response to an insult
54 Turns sharply
55 Alert formally
58 Cavern sound
59 Dr. Pavlov
60 Harm's way
61 Hamelin evictees
62 Do lab work
63 Send to another team

DOWN

1 Brings up the rear
2 Touched down
3 ___ voce
4 From now on
5 Rule, for short
6 British china

7 Good thing
8 Bard's nightfall
9 Lincoln alternative
10 Pushes roughly
11 Assume leadership
12 Roomy dress
13 Borscht veggies
18 Depend (on)
23 Playwright Simon
25 "Not to mention ..."
26 Nasty-smelling
27 Up to the task
28 Proper name, for example
29 Run away
30 Play parts
32 Memento

34 Drought ender
35 Imitative bird
37 Improvising
38 One asking questions
40 Adorable
41 Floral welcome
43 Rodeo ropes
44 In a bit
45 Crystal ball user
46 Author Jong
47 Bloodhound's lead
49 NASA spacewalks
51 Turkish money
52 The "A" in DNA
53 Soccer legend
56 "___ had it!"
57 Make a choice

★★ A Froggy Day

Enter the maze from the right as indicated by the arrow, pass through all the stars exactly once each, then exit at the top. You may not retrace your path.

Say It Again

What four-letter word can be either a sporting venue or a group of dishonest people?

___ ___ ___ ___

Fill in the blank squares so that every row, column, 3×3 box, *and* each of the 3×3 gray regions contains the digits 1 through 9 exactly once each.

				2				8
			7					
8			5		6	2		
		1			5		3	
	5	9	1					
	7	6	3		4		1	9
	1		9	4				
7			2					
		2						5

M I X A G R A M S

Each line contains a five-letter word and a four-letter word that have been mixed together. (The order of the letters in each word has not been changed.) Unmix the two words on each line and write them in the spaces provided. For example, D A R I U N V E T = DRIVE + AUNT. When you're done, find a two-part answer to the clue by reading down two letter columns in the answers.

CLUE: Tackle's teammate

I N C U F E R B E = _ _ _ _ _ + _ _ _ _

F L U S T A T E R = _ _ _ _ _ + _ _ _ _

T A M E C L E K E = _ _ _ _ _ + _ _ _ _

S O A P L K I T S = _ _ _ _ _ + _ _ _ _

★★★ Car Wear by Fred Piscop

ACROSS

1 Iconic riveter
6 Crows' cries
10 Turner of rock
14 Antitheft device
15 Natural soother
16 Mineral in lentils
17 "Understand?"
18 Baby powder mineral
19 Sail holder
20 Transmission lever
22 Answer to "That so?"
23 Gal's pal
24 Mean and nasty
26 Burrowing rodent
30 Parsley unit
32 Blunted sword
33 What's inevitable
35 NBA's sport, for short
39 Purple shade
41 Actor Stiller
42 Photo tint
43 Brief tussle
44 Sausage unit
46 Manor bigwig
47 Actress Barkin
49 Take-home amount
51 Written for voices
54 Sailor's milieu
55 Leveling strip
56 Part of a car-slowing device
62 Concerning
63 Roof edge

64 Add up
66 Beehive State athletes
67 Like true fans
68 Wipe clean
69 Ticked off
70 Loch of note
71 Direct attention

DOWN

1 Fine stationery
2 Cassini of fashion
3 Fill past full
4 ___ la Douce
5 Come into view
6 Noseless comics character
7 Jai ___

8 Pack animal
9 Zone
10 Engine valve regulator
11 Ticked off
12 Emphatic denial
13 Unable to sit still
21 Ride the waves
25 Barbecue fare
26 Solidifies
27 Mayberry tyke
28 Hit, as with hailstones
29 Temperature-regulating conduit
30 Brew holder
31 Ivy League school
34 Up to the task
36 Each

37 Pre-euro unit
38 Noblewoman
40 Fast food drink
45 Patella site
48 Mail-order giant
50 Bonnet time
51 Yuletide name
52 Can't help but
53 Riverbank frolicker
54 Depot postings, for short
57 Boffo review
58 Hertz rival
59 Aesopian loser
60 Norwegian saint
61 Choice word
65 "So's ___ old man!"

★★ One-Way Streets

The map below represents a set of intersecting streets on which a road rally is taking place. The black squares represent checkpoints. The S's stand for "start" and "stop," but which is which is left for you to determine. You must find a route that starts at one S, passes through all checkpoints exactly once, and ends at the other S. Arrows indicate one-way traffic for that block only. No intersection may be entered more than once.

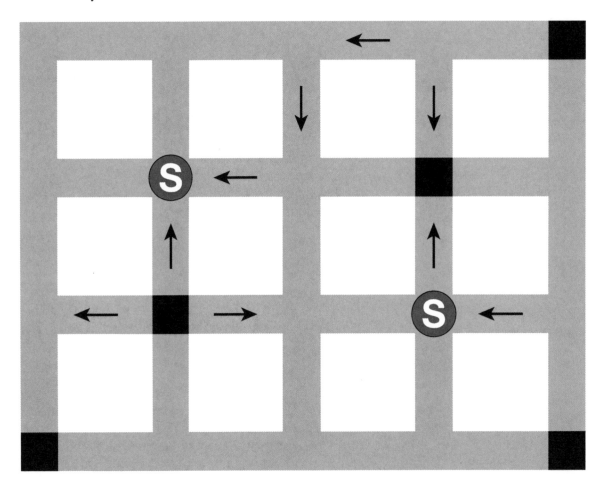

Sound Thinking

Common words whose consonant sounds are SH, R, and D (once each, in that order) include SHEARED and ASSURED. What other seven-letter word that isn't a verb is pronounced with the same consonant sounds in the same order?

_____

★★ Star Search

Can you find the stars hidden in some of the blank squares? Numbered squares indicate how many stars are hidden in the squares adjacent to them in any direction (including diagonally). There is never more than one star in any square.

		3			1		1		
	4		3	2				3	
	3	5					2		2
		3		3	2				2
	3	2				2		3	3
	1				2				
						1			
				2					

C H O I C E   W O R D S

Form three six-letter words from the same category by selecting one letter from each column three times. Each letter will be used exactly once.

Example: B A B C O T   Answer: BOBCAT, JAGUAR, OCELOT
          J O E U A R
          O C G L A T

    B R E A R E   _ _ _ _ _ _

    C A N N G A   _ _ _ _ _ _

    O H A R N Y   _ _ _ _ _ _

★★★ Contain Yourself by Shirley Soloway

ACROSS

1 Corn product
5 Perfidious
10 Campus hotshot: Abbr.
14 Car toll unit, often
15 Bagel flavor
16 Monaco money
17 Overpowering force
19 Ripening agent
20 "To Autumn," for one
21 Eshkol successor
22 Odin, for one
24 Poker ploy
26 Official language of India
27 Stamp collector's envelope
29 Seahawks' div.
32 Studio staff
35 Consider, with "on"
36 Scroll and Key member
37 Very narrow width
38 "No seats today"
39 Exam for jrs.
40 Mark, as a ballot
41 Biblical twin
43 Espionage expert
45 Lodging place
46 Kitchen feature
48 Sniffed distractions
50 Actor's aide
54 Cuspid
56 Unskilled worker
57 *Pulp Fiction* name
58 Deception

59 Narrow entrance
62 Negate
63 Make cheery
64 Nantes notion
65 Existed
66 Weapon with dartlike electrodes
67 Wine sediment

DOWN

1 Highly significant
2 Radiate
3 *Luck and Pluck* author
4 Tripod part
5 Predicted
6 "___ Song" (John Denver tune)
7 Untrustworthy one
8 Pittance
9 Twist around
10 Part of an Uncle Sam costume
11 High humidity
12 Sweet sandwich
13 Firewood measure
18 *South Pacific* hero
23 Over again
25 Taj Mahal city
26 Informal greeting
28 Cancel, so to speak
30 Dog door, often
31 Charlotte or Sydney
32 Prepare to fly
33 Overproud

34 Battle barrage
38 Drains
39 Brake accessories
41 B-school subject
42 It's a lock
43 "Fa-la-la ..." singer
44 Actress Dunne
47 *Swan Lake* character
49 Mason partner
51 Type of leather
52 Intro speaker
53 Tools with tines
54 Freshwater fish
55 Outstanding
56 Sch. auxiliaries
60 Slangy suffix
61 Zero

★★ Sequence Maze

Enter the maze at bottom right, pass through all the colored squares exactly once each, then exit, all without retracing your path. Your path must alternate between red and blue squares. (The first square you visit may be either red or blue.)

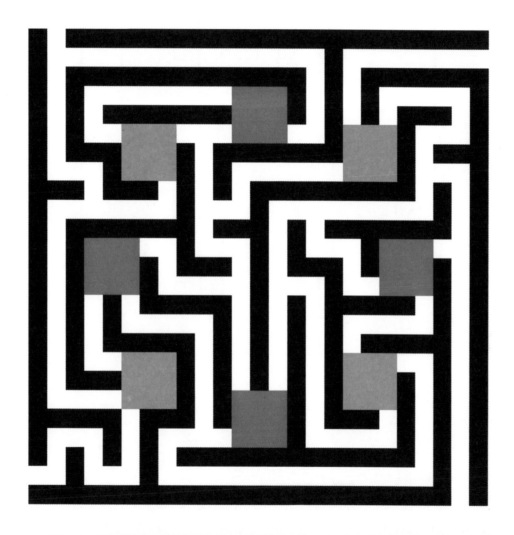

Small Change

Change one letter in each of these two words to form a common two-word phrase. For example, PANTRY CHEW becomes PASTRY CHEF.

LATER CAVE

_____

★★ Sudoku

Fill in the blank squares so that every row, column, and 3×3 box contains the digits 1 through 9 exactly once each.

				5	6			
		9		1		5		
	6		3	7			1	
		8			1			4
7	3	2				6	8	1
5			7			9		
	1			2	7		9	
		4		8		3		
			4	9				

CENTURY MARKS

Select one number in each of the four columns so that the total adds up to exactly 100.

For example:

$$\boxed{\frac{6}{\;\;8\;\;}} + \boxed{\frac{15}{73}} + \boxed{\frac{40}{61}} + \boxed{\frac{29}{37}} = 100$$

$$\boxed{\frac{19}{34}} + \boxed{\frac{15}{29}} + \boxed{\frac{39}{28}} + \boxed{\frac{13}{26}} = 100$$

★★★ Think Fast by Shirley Soloway

ACROSS

1 Herring relative
5 Honolulu-based detective
9 Caustic
14 Scottish philosopher
15 Leaf projection
16 Irish county
17 It means "both"
18 Imitative one
19 Trade shows
20 Mercury alias
23 Squid weapon
24 One way up
25 Fix deeply
27 Roof angles
30 Kid's crude telephone
33 Tanning lotion stats
37 Give a ticket to
39 Nonpaying activity
40 Hard to believe
41 Mother of Isaac
43 Escalator maker
44 Had pot luck, perhaps
46 Gambling game
47 Caustic solutions
48 Cut again, as a film
50 Stratagem
52 Computer help-line workers
54 Marinara alternative
58 Scratch up
60 Idioms, for example
64 Pass, as a bill
66 Light melody
67 The Andrews Sisters, e.g.

68 Engine part
69 Not playing today
70 Starting
71 Hostile state
72 Pull apart
73 Writer Jaffe

DOWN

1 NBA star, familiarly
2 Soil enricher
3 Circumference
4 Use salt on, perhaps
5 English Lit study
6 Arizona Indian
7 Explorer Tasman
8 Courage
9 Biting, as criticism
10 XVI × X
11 Hub of the Black Hills
12 Gate material
13 Work place
21 Eur. speedometer reading
22 911 responder
26 Register
28 French cabaret star
29 Watchband
31 Friendly *femme*
32 Costner role
33 Main attraction
34 Expensive spread
35 Car dealer's discount
36 Decline

38 Anthony Eden title
42 1-Down, for one
45 Encouraging words
49 Cinema sound system
51 "No question"
53 Of two minds
55 Hindustani instrument
56 Piece of sculpture
57 Bagel flavoring
58 Insignificant
59 Poetic adverb
61 Take the bus
62 ___ *Enchanted* (Anne Hathaway film)
63 Parlor piece
65 Dot follower

★★ Split Decisions

In this crossword puzzle with no clues, each answer consists of two words whose spellings are the same except for the pairs of consecutive letters given. All answers are common words (no phrases), and none are hyphenated; one is a common capitalized word. Some individual clues may have more than one solution, but only one word pair will correctly link up with all other word pairs.

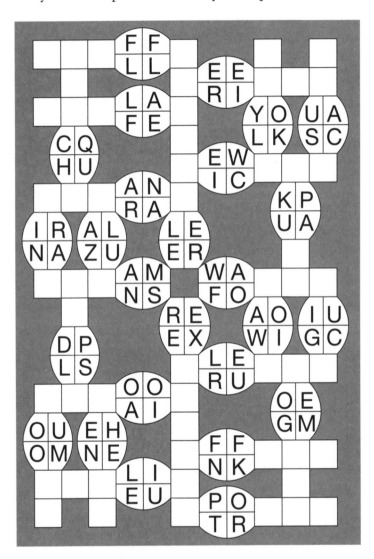

Transdeletion

Delete one letter from the word TSUNAMI and anagram the rest to get a U.S. state capital.

_____

★★ Number-Out

Shade squares so that no number appears in any row or column more than once. Shaded squares may not touch each other horizontally or vertically, and all unshaded squares must form a single continuous area.

1	4	3	6	5	3
3	5	5	4	1	4
2	5	3	4	1	1
4	5	1	4	2	3
2	6	4	1	3	5
6	3	5	5	5	2

Who's What Where?

The correct term for a resident of Allentown, Pennsylvania, is:

A) Allenite

B) Allentowner

C) Allentonian

D) Allentownite

Think Alike

Unscramble the letters in the phrase ERODE OVAL to form two words with the same or similar meanings. For example, BEST RATING can be anagrammed to spell START and BEGIN.

_____   _____

★★★ Prize Cries by Norma Steinberg

ACROSS

1 Go separate ways
5 Health resorts
9 Speak derisively
14 History, so to speak
15 Actress Turner
16 Wanderer
17 Section for Masses
18 Letters on a memo
19 Singer Baker
20 Cry on a warship
23 Throng
24 Noah's handiwork
25 Cry out loud
28 It's west of Que.
29 Wee
33 "Okay!"
34 Jeweled crown
35 Gin joint inventory
36 Cry from the bleachers
40 Worker's incentive
41 Navigator
42 Got up
43 Come home exhausted
45 Cookie Monster's home
48 Poetic work
49 NOW project
50 For rent
52 Cry from the bus driver
57 Snake charmer's snake
59 Lamb's pen name
60 Take at the arena
61 Poe's middle name
62 Rec rooms
63 Auction advisory
64 Orange covers
65 Portnoy's creator
66 Trawler equipment

DOWN

1 Waterproof cloak
2 Funicello's frequent costar
3 Go back
4 Part of a tire
5 Thin board
6 Hiking trail
7 One chip, perhaps
8 Beach shoe
9 Bite to eat
10 Bop
11 What's left out
12 About 4% of whole milk
13 Pharmaceutical-regulating agcy.
21 Depends (on)
22 "... ___ he drove out of sight"
26 Eleven, in Lyons
27 Quilters' convocation
30 Author Fleming
31 Capote, to friends
32 St. Pete neighbor
33 Start of a street
34 Factual
35 Eyre's creator
36 Cherry or walnut
37 String quartet, e.g.
38 Quite generous
39 Yale student
40 Sis's sibling
43 "Dr." of rap
44 Not for kids
45 Tickle
46 "Get lost!"
47 Tension
49 *The American Century* author
51 Choir accompaniment
53 Spoken
54 Muffin topping
55 Hue
56 Leftovers dish
57 Dental work
58 "Go, matador!"

Enter the letters A, B, and C into the diagram, filling in some (but not all) of the squares so that each row and column contains each letter exactly once. The letters outside the diagram indicate the first letter encountered in the indicated row or column when moving in the direction of the arrow from that side of the grid.

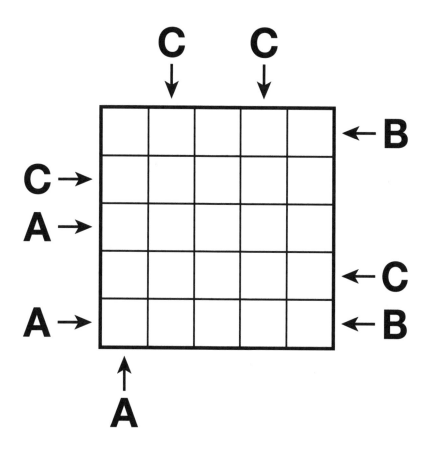

Three of a Kind

Find a set of three hidden words in the sentence that go together in some way. For example, "Chefs were **bus**ily slicing **car**rots and **cab**bage" conceals the set "bus, car, cab."

So, let's search for the elusive buried treasure.

★★ Find the Ships

Ten ships of four different sizes (shown below left) are hidden in the diagram. Ships may be oriented horizontally or vertically, and may not touch each other, not even diagonally. A square containing wavy lines represents open water; such a square will not contain any part of a ship. Numbers at the edge of the diagram indicate how many squares in that row or column contain parts of ships, including any which may have already been placed as clues.

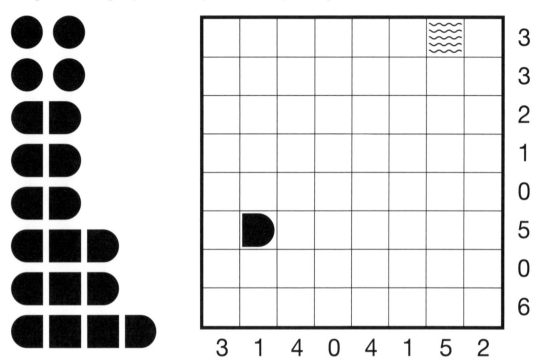

Two-by-Four

The eight letters in the word DRUDGERY can be rearranged in only one way to form a pair of common four-letter words. Can you find them?

__ __ __ __   __ __ __ __

★★★ Line Drawing

Draw two straight lines from edge to edge to make four regions, each containing five letters, such that the groups of letters can be anagrammed to make four related five-letter words.

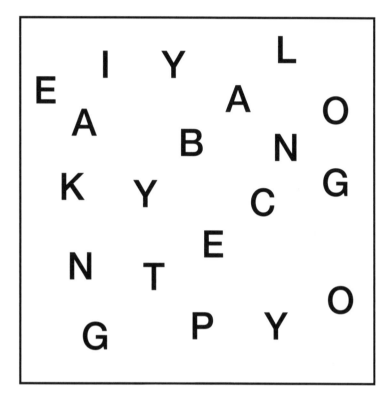

CLUELESS CROSSWORD

Complete the crossword with common, uncapitalized seven-letter words, based on the letters already filled in for you.

★★★ High Spirits by Shirley Soloway

ACROSS

1 Cosmetics applicator
5 Hacienda brick
10 Provoke to anger
14 Vegetable spread
15 Tibetan monks
16 Vanderbilt or Rockefeller: Abbr.
17 Hammerstein collaborator
18 See 19-Across
19 With 18-Across, prepare
20 Stamping out
22 Dogpatch denizen
23 Mauna ___
24 Luxurious
26 Bridal gown attachment
29 Parish priest
31 Apple varieties
33 Latter-day greeting
37 Wall St. debut
38 Bea Arthur sitcom
40 Baltimore paper
41 Combine against, with "on"
44 Corned beef partner
47 Mosaic features
49 House members of a sort
50 Laser device
53 Hack
54 Group's jargon
55 French Quarter addr.
61 ___ breve
62 Our, to Renoir
63 Travel with a band
64 Overflow
65 Cells for sailors
66 ___-European languages
67 Art Deco artist
68 Even-temperedness, e.g.
69 Bottom line

DOWN

1 Lo mein cookers
2 Actor Guinness
3 Galba's predecessor
4 "Be straight with me!"
5 ___ Centauri
6 Flamboyant surrealist
7 Yemen neighbor
8 Stephen King's home
9 Half a figure eight
10 Sounded like thunder
11 Not sensible
12 Compare
13 Seven-time French Open champ
21 Swindles
22 Airport rental
25 Cash recipient
26 Piece of kindling
27 Morning TV cohost
28 Soon, to Spenser
29 Bks. examiner
30 Loan shark's crime
32 More than adequate
34 Laptop lugger
35 Couple
36 Furthest points
39 Prefix for function
42 Card-playing session
43 Golden Rule word
45 Spill a secret
46 Far from creative
48 Shady spots
50 Dinnerware piece
51 Machinery maintenance person
52 Shoreline feature
53 High point
56 Elevator name
57 Lobby for
58 Improper act
59 Beer, so to speak
60 Move briskly
62 Lakers' league

★★ Looped Path

Draw a continuous, unbroken loop that passes through all of the red, blue, and white squares exactly once each. You may move from square to square horizontally or vertically, but never diagonally, and the path must alternate passing through red and blue squares (with any number of white squares in between). Two parts of the loop have been drawn in for you in gray.

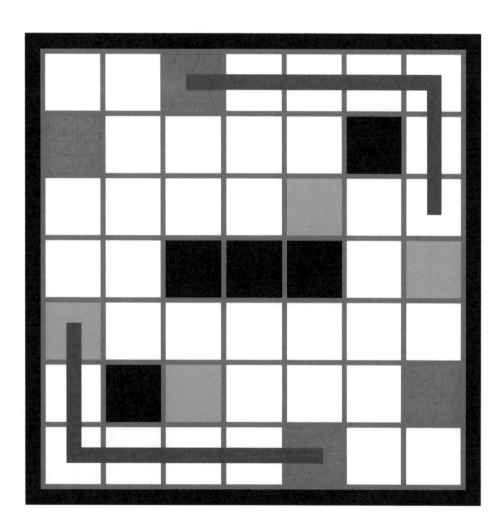

Betweener

What four-letter word can go between the two words below so that it forms compound words with both the word preceding it and the word following it?

OAT __ __ __ __ **TIME**

Fill in the blank squares so that every row, column, 3×3 box, *and* each of the 3×3 gray regions contains the digits 1 through 9 exactly once each.

					7			
	3	8					2	9
			9			6		1
						3		
1		3						8
	5					4		
					5	9		
		1			2	8		
	7	4			3			5

M I X A G R A M S

Each line contains a five-letter word and a four-letter word that have been mixed together. (The order of the letters in each word has not been changed.) Unmix the two words on each line and write them in the spaces provided. For example, D A R I U N V E T = DRIVE + AUNT. When you're done, find a multipart answer to the clue by reading down two letter columns in the answers.

CLUE: Ignore Bart's advice

C A T C H E R A Y = _ _ _ _ _ + _ _ _ _

A S K I S A C K Y = _ _ _ _ _ + _ _ _ _

S O U P L O V E N = _ _ _ _ _ + _ _ _ _

E G G R O W E N T = _ _ _ _ _ + _ _ _ _

ACROSS

1 Removes the rough spots from
6 Coal carrier
10 Strong wind
14 Insurance paperwork
15 Space prefix
16 Nike alternative
17 Excessive
18 Noggin
19 Impolite look
20 Civil War event
23 One or more
24 Vietnam neighbor
25 Cry to a calf
26 "Shall we?" response
27 Alley game
31 "Blue ___" (Berlin tune)
34 Untold centuries
35 Artist Lichtenstein
36 Biblical phrase
41 Ginnie or Fannie follower
42 Become rancid
43 Sports surprise
44 3-D
47 Exams for srs.
49 Big bird of myth
50 "Now ___ this!"
51 Romance
54 Potent punch, perhaps
59 Circular path
60 Huff and puff
61 Salami variety
62 As well
63 Savvy about
64 Antagonist
65 Huskies' load
66 Hardy heroine
67 Prescribed amounts

DOWN

1 Diver's gear
2 Historian Nevins
3 Dapper
4 Gossip
5 Most diminutive
6 Social no-nos
7 Shoals
8 Kuwaiti, for one
9 Enduring symbol
10 Horse's gait
11 State with certainty
12 Stead
13 Be deserving of
21 Erode, with "into"
22 Contemporary of Bela and Boris
26 Luau neckwear
27 "Little piggie"
28 S&L offerings
29 Narrow margin of victory
30 Part of CBS
31 Houston et al.
32 Sack start
33 Creative contribution
34 Rescue squad member: Abbr.
37 Eccentric one
38 "You've got mail" co.
39 In a lather
40 Second ltr. addendum
45 Stand of a sort
46 Accelerator bit
47 Shouting matches
48 "That's nice!"
50 Indirect indications
51 Cellar selections
52 Carol start
53 Gives the thumbs-up
54 Word of regret
55 Helpful person
56 Repeated word heard in a Stein line
57 Taper off
58 Card-marking game

★★★ Fences

Connect the dots with vertical or horizontal lines so that a single loop is formed with no crossings or branches. Each number indicates how many lines surround it; squares with no number may be surrounded by any number of lines.

```
2          2 2    3

      3
   0       3         2
   3                 2
 1                 3
 2       2         0
          0
 1     1 1           3
```

Wrong Is Right

Which of these four words is misspelled?

A) clandestine   B) clairvoyance

C) claustrophobia   D) clavacle

★★ Dotty

Draw a line traveling from square to square, moving horizontally or vertically (but never diagonally), that visits every square exactly once. You may move from one square to another only if it contains a dot of the same color and size. For instance, from the top left corner you could move to the right (since that square contains a small red dot) or down (since that square contains a large red dot).

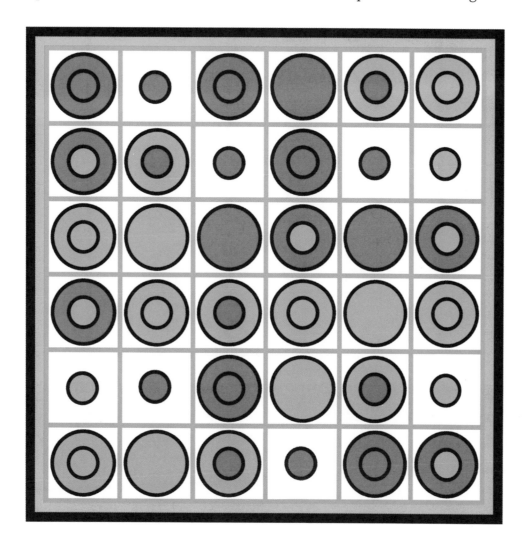

Say It Again

What four-letter word can be either a type of mammal or a verb meaning "close"?

___ ___ ___ ___

★★ Number-Out

Shade squares so that no number appears in any row or column more than once. Shaded squares may not touch each other horizontally or vertically, and all unshaded squares must form a single continuous area.

3	6	2	1	5	5
2	4	4	4	3	6
4	2	5	6	1	1
3	3	3	5	2	1
1	4	6	4	2	2
5	1	2	3	6	6

In Other Words

There is only one common uncapitalized word that contains the consecutive sequence of letters XIR. What is the word?

_____

Think Alike

Unscramble the letters in the phrase LOB ADVERB to form two words with the same or similar meanings. For example, BEST RATING can be anagrammed to spell START and BEGIN.

_____   _____

★★★ Principal Sounds by Randall J. Hartman

ACROSS

1 Apt. manager
5 Sentry's place
9 Type of convent
14 Norwegian port
15 Not for
16 Incite
17 Peruse (through)
18 Spotted
19 Land of the Sphinx
20 Eastern capital
23 College in Troy, NY
24 ___ Aviv
25 Deny
29 Gung-ho
31 Utensils for Emeril
33 School gp.
34 Kitchen cover
36 Scorch
37 Ship's personnel
38 Chinese restaurant order
41 Skyline obscurer
42 32-Down bash
43 Chestnut horses
44 Compass reading
45 Gemini, for one
46 Follow the orders of
47 Cherub's superior
49 Claimed the blue ribbon
50 Actress Longoria
53 Sea
57 Cabinet department
60 "___ Lang Syne"
61 "Great Caesar's ghost!"
62 Wide awake
63 Dracula portrayer Lugosi
64 *Vogue* competitor
65 Fender-bender results
66 Leave in stitches
67 Mrs. Dick Tracy

DOWN

1 Like some energy
2 Exhaust
3 Prose appropriator
4 Soybean product
5 Attached with glue
6 Name on Shaq's jersey
7 Pipe piece
8 Fey of *30 Rock*
9 Hockey venues
10 One over par
11 Wall Street order
12 Uncommon sense
13 To date
21 Public outcry
22 Emcee's remarks
26 Emblem of the United States
27 Had dinner at home
28 Looks bored
30 Sotto ___
31 State tree of Texas
32 Home of Diamond Head
34 Signs of soreness
35 Terrible twos, e.g.
36 Close-fitting
37 "Let's go!"
39 Yale who helped found Yale
40 Dry with a twist
45 Has on
46 Calendar column heading
48 Cancel, as a mission
49 Author Cather
51 Small bottles
52 Llama habitat
54 Pinches
55 Two-person contest
56 Comply with
57 Young fellow
58 Microbrewery product
59 Oscar winner as Mohandas

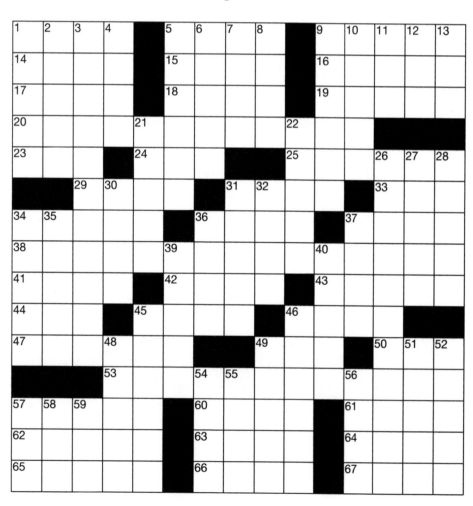

Fill in the diagram so that each rectangular piece contains the digits 1, 2, and 3 once each, according to these rules: 1) No two horizontally or vertically adjacent squares can contain the same digit.
2) Each completed row and column of the diagram must have an equal number of 1's, 2's, and 3's.

Two-by-Four

The eight letters in the word PIQUANCY can be rearranged in only one way to form a pair of common four-letter words. Can you find them?

__ __ __ __   __ __ __ __

Ten ships of four different sizes (shown below left) are hidden in the diagram. Ships may be oriented horizontally or vertically, and may not touch each other, not even diagonally. A square containing wavy lines represents open water; such a square will not contain any part of a ship. Numbers at the edge of the diagram indicate how many squares in that row or column contain parts of ships, including any which may have already been placed as clues.

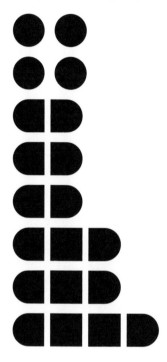

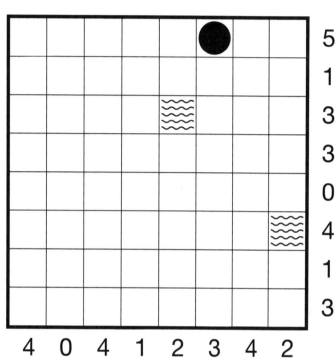

S U D O K U S U M

Fill in the missing digits from 1 to 9 so that each is used once and the sum of each row and column is as indicated.

Example:

	12	14	19
6			3
17	6		
22		8	

Answer:

	12	14	19
6	1	2	3
17	6	4	7
22	5	8	9

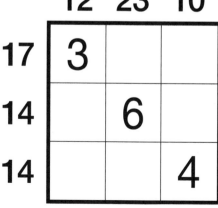

ACROSS

1 Loud noise
5 Superficial shine
10 Nautical mop
14 A great distance
15 Devilfish
16 "Goodness!"
17 Fast-moving object
19 Existence
20 Actress Allen
21 *Bus Stop* playwright
22 Cash-spewing devices
23 Carry ___ (sing OK)
24 Suffix for block
25 Exist
26 Finest possible
28 Flavor enhancer initials
30 Eat in the evening
33 *Rules of Order* guy
36 Note the differences between
38 Kans. neighbor
39 Nasal appraisal
41 *Born Free* lioness
42 Still shrink-wrapped
44 Sound system controls
46 Cul-de-___
47 Infomercials, for example
48 Mongrels
49 Answer sheet
51 Argentine aunt
53 Internet commerce
57 Research centers
59 Accrue income

60 Household help
61 Summer snack
62 Brain
64 Singer Fitzgerald
65 Columbus's hometown
66 Limerick's land
67 Customs payment
68 Virtuous one
69 Speedsters of yore

DOWN

1 Raisiny cake
2 G sharp alias
3 Pacific island nation
4 Podded veggie
5 BBC clock setting
6 Cowpoke's catcher
7 Without letup
8 Rose in *Gypsy*, e.g.
9 Benefit
10 Alternative power
11 January retail event
12 Two-band
13 Tourney passes
18 Mean look
25 Performer's rep.
27 Rise
29 Major mess
31 Sputnik launcher
32 Bake sale sponsors
33 Steals from
34 Cajun cookery ingredient

35 Dojo designation
36 Female seal
37 Idaho and Iowa, in 2004
40 Parkway stop
43 Calendar box
45 Battleground
48 Steep-sided valley
50 Editorial piece
52 Farsi speaker
54 Those against
55 Not moving
56 Ancient strings
57 Wasn't candid
58 Rights org.
59 Dairy dozen
63 Feet-wiping place

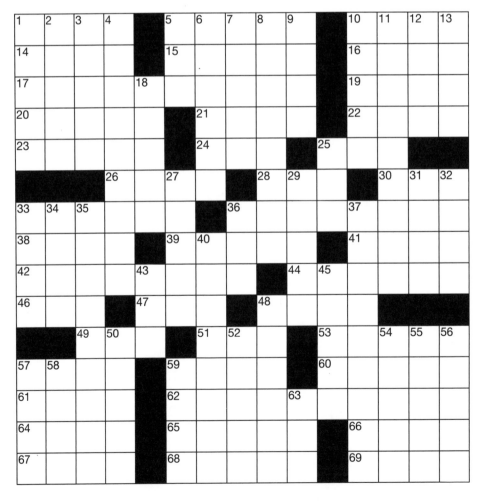

★★ Alternating Tiles

Starting at one of the red tiles at the top of the diagram and moving one square at a time either horizontally or vertically (but never diagonally), always alternating between red and yellow tiles, find the shortest path through the tiles to the bottom.

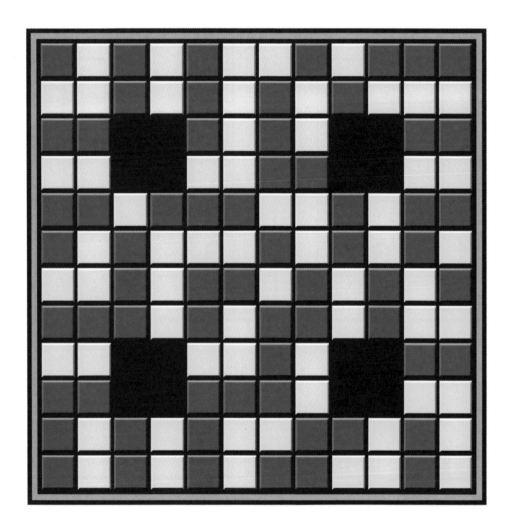

Small Change

Change one letter in each of these two words to form a common two-word phrase. For example, PANTRY CHEW becomes PASTRY CHEF.

FAIL STAKE

Can you find the stars hidden in some of the blank squares? Numbered squares indicate how many stars are hidden in the squares adjacent to them in any direction (including diagonally). There is never more than one star in any square.

CHOICE WORDS

Form three six-letter words from the same category by selecting one letter from each column three times. Each letter will be used exactly once.

Example: B A B C O T   Answer: BOBCAT, JAGUAR, OCELOT
         J O E U A R
         O C G L A T

    A B R N U R   _ _ _ _ _ _

    G A C R E N   _ _ _ _ _ _

    O C T A I E   _ _ _ _ _ _

★★★ Trunk Lines by Shirley Soloway

ACROSS

1 Nigeria neighbor
5 NBA team, in headlines
10 Ancient Persian poet
14 Seward Peninsula city
15 City on the Missouri
16 Play in a pool
17 Radar screen image
18 Mideast capital
19 Monumental
20 Iowa city
23 Grazing land
24 Spanish article
25 Gather
27 Most spacious
32 Some loaves
33 61-Down dances
34 Roman moon goddess
36 Turned brown, perhaps
39 Leaving stat.
40 *Arabian Nights* character
43 Feel bad about
44 Nastase contemporary
46 French state
47 Bedroom community
49 Gung-ho about
51 Vulnerable position
53 *Tosca* composer
56 Strand in a cell
57 Comic strip exclamation
58 Schwarzenegger nickname, with "the"
64 Horn sound
66 Pretexts
67 Social engagement
68 Concerning
69 Fishing author Walton
70 "Horrors!"
71 Kind of quartz
72 Irascible
73 Tries to collect damages

DOWN

1 *Fast Money* network
2 Logical flaw
3 In the thick of
4 *The Untouchables* director
5 Lacking etiquette
6 Austen novel
7 End table item
8 Bangkok residents
9 Shoreline crustacean
10 Be in 38-Down
11 French toast topping
12 Parting word
13 Summation
21 Mrs. Gorbachev
22 "Wait a minute!"
26 Spectrum shade
27 Ostrich relative
28 On the ___ (not speaking)
29 Jackson nickname
30 Skirt feature
31 Heavy instruments
35 Brussels-based org.
37 Brussels bread
38 Obligation
41 *Trinity* author
42 MetLife rival
45 Env. insertion
48 Tic-tac-toe symbols
50 Argentine aunt
52 Frolicsome
53 Backyard area
54 NCAA Division I team
55 Japanese automaker
59 Romanov ruler
60 Authentic
61 Diamond Head locale
62 "Don't throw bouquets ___"
63 Piano parts
65 Cowboy nickname

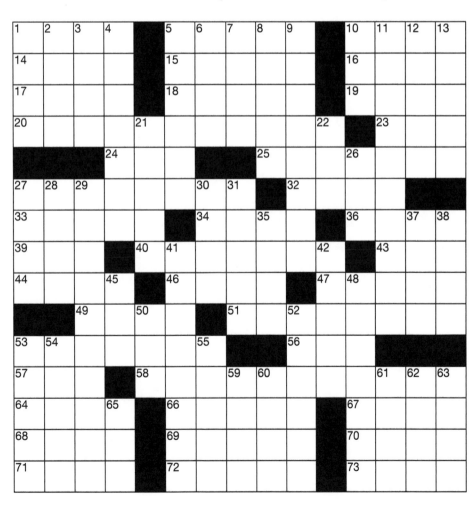

Fill in the blank squares so that every row, column, and 3×3 box contains the digits 1 through 9 exactly once each.

2							8	1
			4	2				
					3			9
	3		8			7		
	4							1
		5			7		9	
9			5					
				4	6			
7		1						2

M I X A G R A M S

Each line contains a five-letter word and a four-letter word that have been mixed together. (The order of the letters in each word has not been changed.) Unmix the two words on each line and write them in the spaces provided. For example, D A R I U N V E T = DRIVE + AUNT. When you're done, find a two-part answer to the clue by reading down two letter columns in the answers.

CLUE: Mecca, for one

S U S C H A R E R = _ _ _ _ _ + _ _ _ _

S A I G O N R E Y = _ _ _ _ _ + _ _ _ _

F I A T L O M M Y = _ _ _ _ _ + _ _ _ _

B I D Y Y E L L S = _ _ _ _ _ + _ _ _ _

The map below represents a set of intersecting streets on which a road rally (starting at A and ending at B) is taking place. The black squares represent checkpoints. You must find a route that starts at A, passes through all checkpoints exactly once, and ends at B. Arrows indicate one-way traffic for that block only. No intersection may be entered more than once.

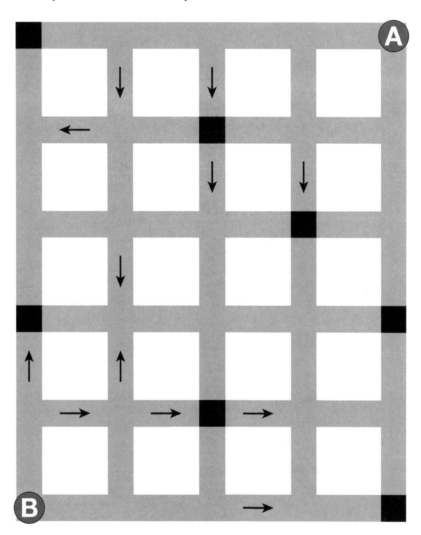

Sound Thinking

What is the only common uncapitalized word whose consonant sounds are S, M, S, T, R, and S, in that order? (It's not SEMESTERS, which ends with a Z sound.)

_____

Enter the letters A, B, and C into the diagram, filling in some (but not all) of the squares so that each row and column contains each letter exactly once. The letters outside the diagram indicate the first letter encountered in the indicated row or column when moving in the direction of the arrow from that side of the grid.

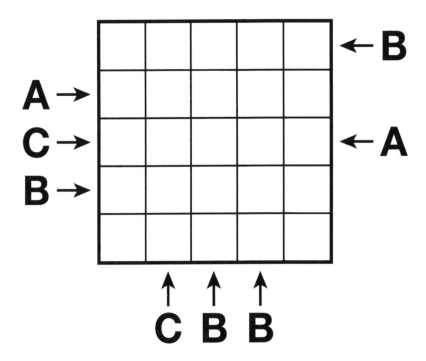

Betweener

What five-letter word can go between the two words below so that it forms compound words with both the word preceding it and the word following it?

AN __ __ __ __ __ **WISE**

National Treasure

There is one common seven-letter word that can be formed from the letters in CAMBODIAN. What is it?

__ __ __ __ __ __ __

★★★ The Usual by Kevin Donovan

ACROSS

1 Hound sounds
5 Ornamental tree
10 Tailless primate
13 Manhattan Project result
15 Some Pennsylvania people
16 Cause disquiet
17 Full-time force
19 Prime period
20 Ocean phenomena
21 Ninety-one, to Nero
22 Swamp thing
23 Sudden intake
25 Cast a spell over
27 And so forth
31 Street tough
32 Sign of summer
33 Cuts, as stems
35 Minuscule creature
38 Explosive noise
39 Freshen, as a drink
41 Garfield's owner
42 Ready for action
45 Warning system
47 Food grain
48 They're found in the ground
50 Flight breaks
52 Some furry friends
55 Informal negative
56 Immense
57 Cube root of eight
59 Advances
62 Union preceder
63 John D. Rockefeller's company
66 River, to Ricardo
67 Adjust
68 Mountie's suit material
69 Pea place
70 Needing a cleaning
71 Old West exclamation

DOWN

1 Ingot shape
2 Help in wrongdoing
3 Toon bear
4 Ink spot
5 "___ out!"
6 CinemaScope successor
7 *The Odyssey* sorceress
8 Reliable moneymaker
9 Reluctant to mingle
10 One of the masses
11 Eva Duarte's married name
12 On the money
14 Sheepish sounds
18 Give the go-ahead
22 Pal
24 Happening earlier
26 Half a dance name
27 Island of exile
28 Flaw in fabric
29 Societal well-being
30 Dismay
34 Khartoum's land
36 Sow's mate
37 Hill residents
40 1950s scandal subject
43 Pennsylvania port
44 Place to relax
46 Cowboys, frequently
49 Come to terms
51 Peddled
52 Chick's noise
53 Video complement
54 Strikes swiftly
58 Snake eyes
60 Kid-vid explorer
61 Roadside reference
63 Retail mogul Walton
64 Like some martinis
65 Journey part

★★★ Find the Ships

Ten ships of four different sizes (shown below left) are hidden in the diagram. Ships may be oriented horizontally or vertically, and may not touch each other, not even diagonally. A square containing wavy lines represents open water; such a square will not contain any part of a ship. Numbers at the edge of the diagram indicate how many squares in that row or column contain parts of ships, including any which may have already been placed as clues.

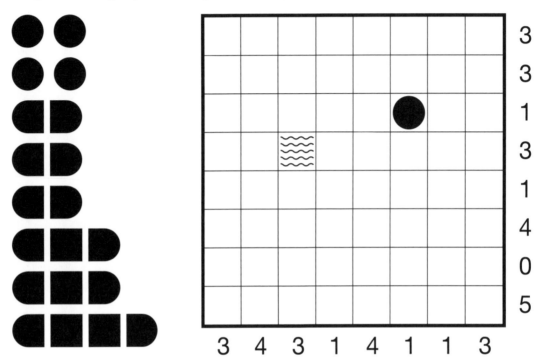

Two-by-Four

The eight letters in the word FURLOUGH can be rearranged in only one way to form a pair of common four-letter words. Can you find them?

___ ___ ___ ___   ___ ___ ___ ___

Fill in the diagram so that each rectangular piece contains the digits 1, 2, and 3 once each, according to these rules: 1) No two horizontally or vertically adjacent squares can contain the same digit. 2) Each completed row and column of the diagram must have an equal number of 1's, 2's, and 3's.

			2					3
					2			
	2							
1							3	
			1					
			3				2	
	1							
					1			

ADDITION SWITCH

Switch the positions of two digits in the incorrect sum at right to get a correct sum. For example, in the incorrect sum 955 + 264 = 411, you would swap the second 1 in 411 with the 9 in 955 to get the correct sum 155 + 264 = 419.

$$\begin{array}{r} 720 \\ +373 \\ \hline 697 \end{array}$$

★★★★ Clean Slate by Doug Peterson

ACROSS

1 Part player
6 Like-minded group
10 Didn't go bad
14 Poet Marianne
15 Bebe Neuwirth Broadway role of 1994
16 Teacher's handout
17 Arabian horses, e.g.
19 Taft's alma mater
20 Job detail
21 Hold
22 Former *Weekend Edition Sunday* host Liane
24 MSN rival
26 Man of morals
27 Bubbly beverage
33 Beat in wrestling
34 Furnishing style
35 See 66-Across
37 Add-ons
39 Sacred ceremonies
41 Hindu melody
42 Some terriers
44 Skin application
46 Syllable of disapproval
47 What the Gateway Arch is made of
50 Seaweed
51 "What'd you say?"
52 Really feeling the heat
54 Fluffy wrap
56 Former CW sitcom
60 ___ & *Stitch*
61 Major Australian watercourse
64 Abreast of

65 Top-drawer
66 With 35-Across, Madonna role
67 UPC elements
68 Trampled
69 Tabloid fave

DOWN

1 Bass boosters
2 Stunning success
3 Ran like heck
4 Freight train unit
5 Chancellorsville combatant
6 Squander
7 State bird of Minnesota

8 Overfamiliar
9 Popular nut
10 Address deliverer
11 Try the patience of
12 Hardly tanned
13 Federal agents
18 Lazybones
23 Memo abbr.
25 Signed off on
26 Finds common ground
27 Relaxing getaways
28 Cuts in a zigzag pattern
29 Mayberry sheriff
30 Spikelike formation
31 Parisian pronoun

32 Renegade
36 L.A. Dodgers' league
38 Flippered critters
40 Move easily
43 Zodiac division
45 East Lansing inst.
48 Annoys persistently
49 Flourish
52 Boo-boo
53 Philbin's partner, once
54 U2 frontman
55 Ran up a tab
57 Dark doings
58 ___ noire
59 Burnoose wearer
62 "... ___ a lender be"
63 Remote button

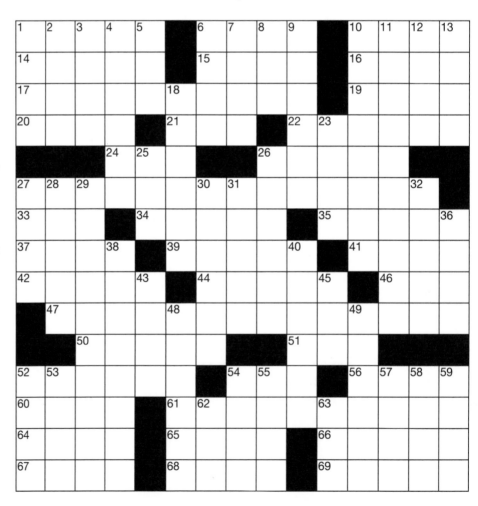

Connect the dots with vertical or horizontal lines so that a single loop is formed with no crossings or branches. Each number indicates how many lines surround it; squares with no number may be surrounded by any number of lines.

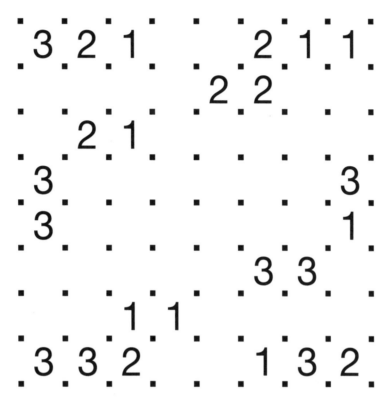

Initial Reaction

Identify the well-known proverb from the first letters of each of its words. For example:
L. B. Y. L. = Look before you leap.

H. A. L. I. B. T. N. _____

Wrong Is Right

Which of these four words is misspelled?

A) eucalyptis

B) euphemism

C) euchre

D) euphonious

Shade squares so that no number appears in any row or column more than once. Shaded squares may not touch each other horizontally or vertically, and all unshaded squares must form a single continuous area.

2	6	4	5	1	3
4	1	3	3	5	6
5	6	2	3	3	5
3	4	5	6	5	3
3	2	5	1	2	4
6	3	5	2	4	1

Think Alike

Unscramble the letters in the phrase FUSSY MOTH to form two words with the same or similar meanings. For example, BEST RATING can be anagrammed to spell START and BEGIN.

_____   _____

ACROSS

1 Slightly
5 Hindu gentleman
10 Kind of lettuce
14 Nobel physicist of 1944
15 Cancel, to NASA
16 Peek follower
17 Author Stoker
18 Prattle
20 Cresting wave
22 Portends
23 Explorers' org.
24 Israel's first U.N. delegate
26 Monastic title
29 Defeat decisively
30 Yank's foe
33 U Thant's birthplace
34 Rum cake
35 Presidential nickname
36 Flighty one
40 Tirana's loc.
41 Nosh
42 Native of Israel
43 Free pass to the next round
44 Main part
45 Yanks' WWII allies
46 Thorn in the side
47 Roll
48 Truckers, at times
51 Checks for drinks
55 Puzzle introduced in 1980
58 Program
60 Atlas, for one
61 Some reeds
62 Common rhyme scheme
63 Manager
64 *The Cosby Show* actress
65 Family members

DOWN

1 Wall Street type
2 Carping remark
3 Construction piece
4 *Goldfinger* device
5 Spongy cake
6 Competent
7 Male bear
8 Eye
9 Wagering spot
10 Industry magnate
11 Bibliography abbr.
12 Femur, for one
13 Some wetlands
19 PayPal parent
21 Take ___ at (attempt)
24 First name in ragtime
25 Crow
26 U.K. sitcom, to fans
27 Intimidate
28 Illegal payoff
29 Eccentric
30 Talmudic scholar
31 Thumbs-up critic
32 Software versions
34 Vow taker
37 Bard's black
38 "Life ___ a dream"
39 New Testament prophet
44 Catch rays
46 Fedora features
47 French seaport
48 Nursery purchase
49 Osso ___
50 Recedes
51 Good, to Garibaldi
52 "... sting like ___"
53 Actress Andersson
54 Thick slice
56 Weep
57 Federal legislation-analysis agcy.
59 Letters on barbells

Enter the grid from the left, pass through all the yellow squares, then exit at right by the shortest possible path. You may only travel horizontally or vertically (never diagonally), and may only turn if the next square in your path is a black square. You may retrace your path, and may make U-turns.

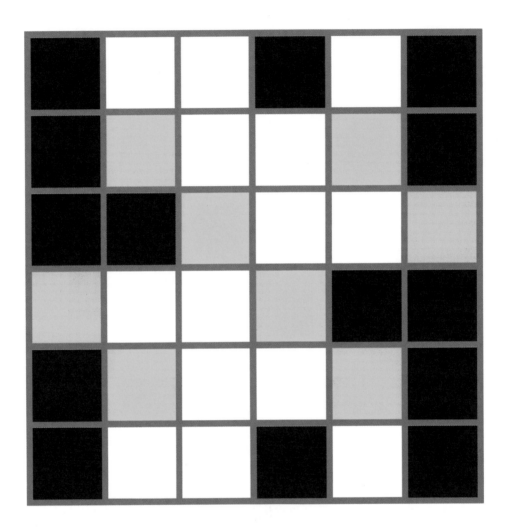

Betweener

What five-letter word can go between the two words below so that it forms compound words with both the word preceding it and the word following it?

TIME __ __ __ __ __ **WORK**

Fill in the blank squares so that every row, column, 3×3 box, *and* each of the 3×3 gray regions contains the digits 1 through 9 exactly once each.

				1			3	
3	8	4			9			
9						8		
			8					5
				2				3
5			4	3		1	2	
	5			7	6			
			3				4	
			9					

M I X A G R A M S

Each line contains a five-letter word and a four-letter word that have been mixed together. (The order of the letters in each word has not been changed.) Unmix the two words on each line and write them in the spaces provided. For example, D A R I U N V E T = DRIVE + AUNT. When you're done, find a multipart answer to the clue by reading down two letter columns in the answers.

CLUE: Quick as a wink

S M O O N I T H C = _ _ _ _ _ + _ _ _ _

S I R C A N I S T = _ _ _ _ _ + _ _ _ _

E M A V E M A N T = _ _ _ _ _ + _ _ _ _

A C H E A R M O L = _ _ _ _ _ + _ _ _ _

★★★★ Labor Paradox? by Robert D. Levin

ACROSS

1 Don't partake
5 English Derby site
10 "Editorially speaking," in a chat room
13 "Hi-yo, Silver" follower
14 Comes closer
15 CAT, for one
16 Start of a riddle
19 Federal medical research agcy.
20 Bar partner
21 Kids' song refrain
22 Do the town
24 Crowd scene participant
25 Fish story
26 100 smackers
28 Doesn't shut up
30 Cologne's water
31 Internet service
34 End of riddle
38 Fuming
39 Navel type
40 Reagan cabinet member
41 Circular
42 Infomercial company
44 Hindu teachers
46 Blake TV role
49 Former Seattle hoopster
50 Gold Coast, today
52 Royal power symbol
53 Answer to riddle
56 Computer customer
57 Black ___ (police van)
58 Guns the engine
59 Something staked
60 The Minutemen
61 Sale condition

DOWN

1 Knight protectors
2 In the least
3 Willie Mays's nickname
4 Charlie Chaplin's brother
5 Gridiron play
6 ___ larceny
7 Political satirist
8 City southwest of Moscow
9 East Lansing sch.
10 More aloof
11 Hyperactive excitement
12 Informed about
15 Clobber, old-style
17 Operatic prince
18 Musical combo
23 ___ doble (Spanish dance)
24 Immeasurable periods
26 Church group
27 Muse count
28 "Delicious!"
29 *Wheel of Fortune* purchase
30 Learning method
31 Call preceders
32 Gstaad gear
33 Part of a tour
35 "Darn it, didn't work!"
36 Fellers
37 1950s Korean leader
41 Tuck, for one
42 Toto's home
43 Mine car
44 Aesopian source of wealth
45 Not achieved
46 Part of a capital-gains calculation
47 Fountain of Rome
48 Bottomless chasm
49 Candle remnant
50 Bewitching, informally
51 Juno's counterpart
54 Second-largest bird
55 "... ___ mouse?"

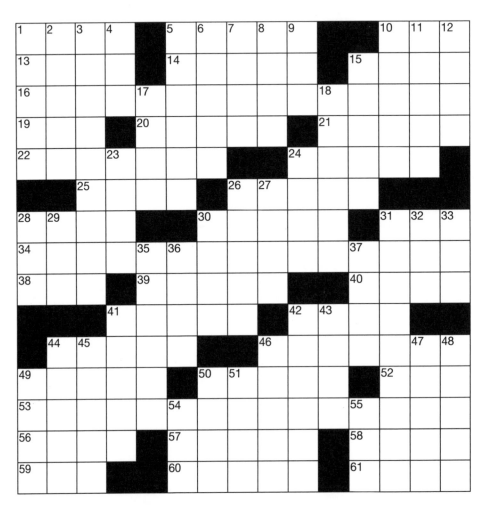

In this crossword puzzle with no clues, each answer consists of two words whose spellings are the same except for the sets of three consecutive letters given. All answers are common words (no phrases), and none are hyphenated or capitalized. Some individual clues may have more than one solution, but only one word pair will correctly link up with all other word pairs.

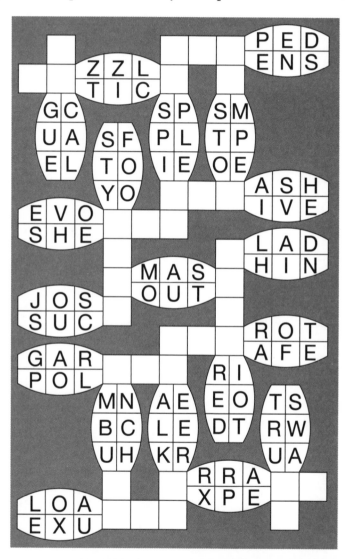

Transdeletion

Delete one letter from the word UNBOILED and anagram the rest to get a long-running comic strip.

_____

The map below represents a set of intersecting streets on which a road rally (starting at A and ending at B) is taking place. The black squares represent checkpoints. You must find a route that starts at A, passes through all checkpoints exactly once, and ends at B. Arrows indicate one-way traffic for that block only. No intersection may be entered more than once.

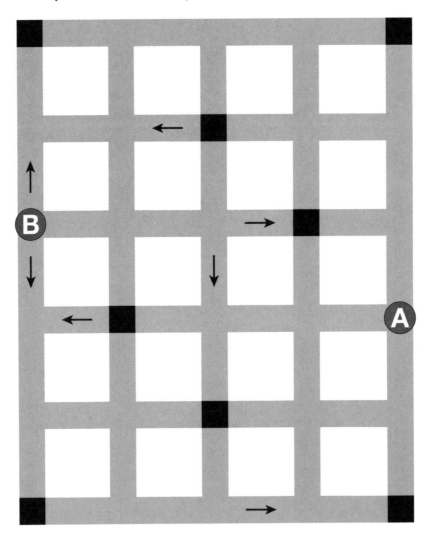

Sound Thinking

The consonant sound in the word T-BOND are T, B, N, and D. What nonhyphenated word is pronounced with the same consonant sounds in the same order?

_____

★★★★ Fall Prelude by Stanley Newman

ACROSS

1 The Eiger, for one
4 Is bold enough
9 Advanced very slowly
14 Carnival locale
15 Writer Calvino
16 What -phile means
17 Poetic adverb
18 Tracking method
19 Santalike
20 Late September event
23 Play the part of
24 Blue Angels org.
25 Illumination source
27 Cheese with a rind
29 Hot tub
32 Fact starter
33 Former New York Philharmonic leader
34 Common Market letters
35 Phrase for late September
39 Grounded bird
40 Takes a lease
41 Roof feature
42 Evidence presenters
43 Race place, familiarly
44 Brunch selections
46 Grasshopper's friend of fable
47 Fabric
48 What late September marks
55 Alfredo alternative
56 Research project
57 Inexperienced
58 Alphabetic quintet
59 Wipe clean
60 MPG rating agcy.
61 Point of view
62 Funnel-shaped
63 For example

DOWN

1 Purview
2 Stead
3 Ominously significant
4 Pretty bad
5 Now
6 Charged towards
7 Mideast carrier
8 Steamed
9 French fumbler of filmdom
10 Marian's love
11 Tied up
12 Cozumel coin
13 Prehistoric predator
21 Destroyed
22 Calls it a day
25 Locked up
26 Oven emanation
27 Wilma Flintstone's pal
28 Greek letters
29 Signals at sea
30 Annoyance
31 Lots of land
33 Heal
36 Take from the attic
37 *Fiddler on the Roof* matchmaker
38 Swimming contests
44 Monty Python member
45 Expressed approval, perhaps
46 Vanya creator
47 House network
48 Books experts
49 Command to Rover
50 Region in Risk
51 Gas group
52 Game like baccarat
53 Northern California county
54 Show flexibility

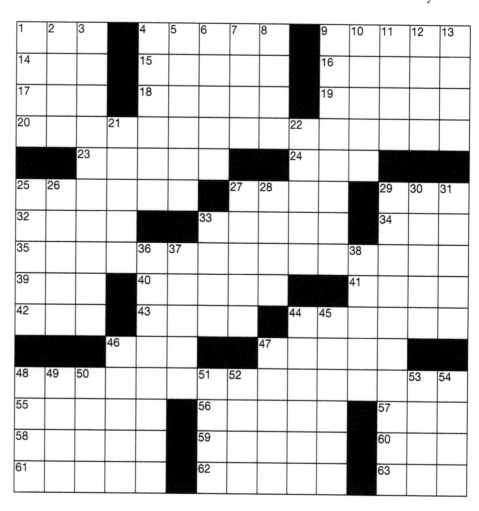

Group the 40 cards below into eight poker hands of five cards each so that each hand contains two pairs or better. The cards in each hand must be connected to each other by common horizontal or vertical sides.

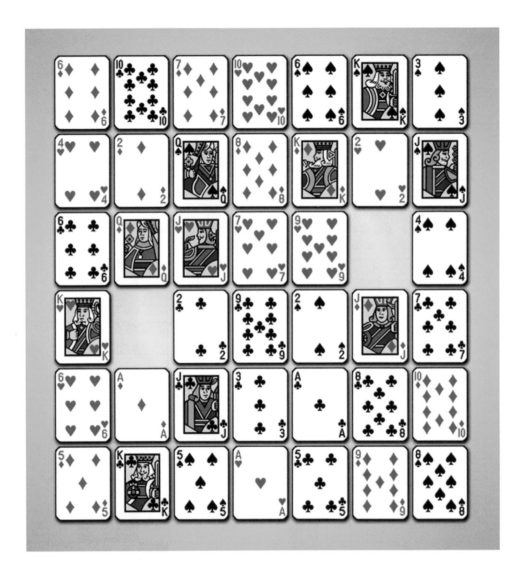

Say It Again

What two five-letter words can each be either a type of vehicle or a verb meaning "instruct"?

___ ___ ___ ___ ___   ___ ___ ___ ___ ___

Can you find the stars hidden in some of the blank squares? Numbered squares indicate how many stars are hidden in the squares adjacent to them in any direction (including diagonally). There is never more than one star in any square.

	1		2		1
1					2
	3		5		1
2				4	
		3		4	
3		6		5	
	3		2	2	

CHOICE WORDS

Form three six-letter words from the same category by selecting one letter from each column three times. Each letter will be used exactly once.

Example: B A B C O T   Answer: BOBCAT, JAGUAR, OCELOT
          J O E U A R
          O C G L A T

C E N A U S   _ _ _ _ _ _

N A R D E N   _ _ _ _ _ _

V A L T I S   _ _ _ _ _ _

Fill in the blank squares so that every row, column, and 3×3 box contains the digits 1 through 9 exactly once each.

						8	2	
1			2	9				
6			7		8			
		4				5	8	
	5						6	
	2	6				3		
			5		4			3
				3	6			1
	1	5						

C E N T U R Y   M A R K S

Select one number in each of the four columns so that the total adds up to exactly 100.

For example: $\dfrac{6}{\boxed{8}}$ + $\dfrac{\boxed{15}}{73}$ + $\dfrac{\boxed{40}}{61}$ + $\dfrac{29}{\boxed{37}}$ = 100

$$\dfrac{36}{18} + \dfrac{50}{23} + \dfrac{37}{13} + \dfrac{28}{14} = 100$$

★★★★ Final Averages by Richard Silvestri

ACROSS

1 Legal rights org.
5 Sentry's cry
9 Sudden feeling of distress
13 Capital of Tibet
15 Stick in the fridge
16 Frankenstein's aide
17 Interpret as
19 Slalom obstacle
20 Run
21 Can't stand
23 Speak like a Castilian
25 Mortise filler
26 Victor's booty
30 Scouting work
33 Nautical starter
34 Sub detector
35 He's on first
38 Nightclub performer
42 Former pullet
43 Sign of spring
44 Cold capital
45 Furniture set
46 Darth Vader, to Luke
48 Lustrous black
51 Love song, at times
53 Friend in crime
56 In the family
61 Uncovered wagon
62 Dessert order
64 *In* ___ (existing)
65 Holy Land line
66 Burn a bit
67 Future specialist
68 Safety devices
69 Turned blue, perhaps

DOWN

1 Female opera villain, often
2 Bloke
3 The Caspian, e.g.
4 Manual consulter
5 Realty listings
6 Maugham title drink
7 Be in charge
8 Time signal
9 Filthy place
10 Encore, literally
11 False
12 Putting place
14 Under any circumstances
18 Elevator innovator
22 Lay away
24 Move on
26 Pageant attire
27 Singer Seeger
28 Setting of *The Plague*
29 Free electron, for one
31 Son of Seth
32 Engine part
34 Rod for roasting
35 Well offering
36 In good shape
37 ___ close to schedule
39 Intimidate
40 Site of the Tell legend
41 Multiplication sign
45 Hunting dog
46 Have a hunch
47 World record?
48 Churchill Downs agenda
49 Humble
50 Guest work
52 Russian range
54 Doing business
55 Rub the wrong way
57 In the thick of
58 *West Side Story* hero
59 Advantage
60 Homeowner's holding
63 Have a hero

Enter the letters A, B, and C into the diagram, filling in some (but not all) of the squares so that each row and column contains each letter exactly once. The letters outside the diagram indicate the first letter encountered in the indicated row or column when moving in the direction of the arrow from that side of the grid.

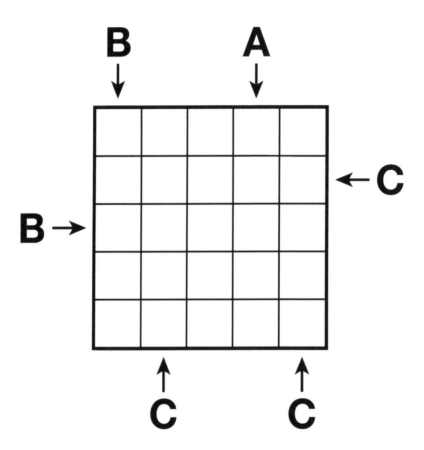

Two-by-Four

The eight letters in the word BEVERAGE can be rearranged in two different ways to form a pair of common four-letter words. Can you find both pairs?

__ __ __ __   __ __ __ __

__ __ __ __   __ __ __ __

Ten ships of four different sizes (shown below left) are hidden in the diagram. Ships may be oriented horizontally or vertically, and may not touch each other, not even diagonally. A square containing wavy lines represents open water; such a square will not contain any part of a ship. Numbers at the edge of the diagram indicate how many squares in that row or column contain parts of ships, including any which may have already been placed as clues.

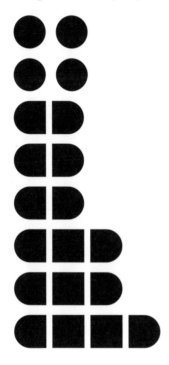

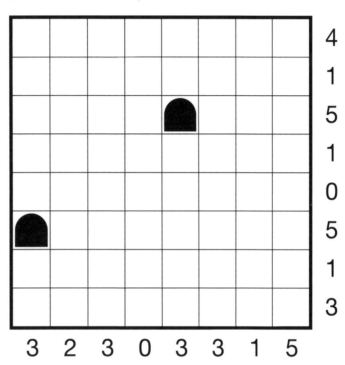

C L U E L E S S C R O S S W O R D

Complete the crossword with common, uncapitalized seven-letter words, based on the letters already filled in for you.

T			A	D		
		N				S
	N	F		N		
		O		T		
V						N
		C				C
	H		A	T		

★★★★ Onion Specific by Merle Baker

ACROSS

1 Family emblem
6 Experts
10 Took a card
14 St. Teresa's town
15 Note-signing transaction
16 Word on some 49-Down coins
17 Mysterious region
20 *Le Monde* article
21 Birds of myth
22 Ready for action
23 Tasman landfall of 1643
24 Financing figs.
25 Hypocritical show
31 Tedious task
32 "___ day goes by ..."
33 Place for a dummy
34 Swindle
35 Half a term for "evenly"
37 Drop off
38 German article
39 *Star Trek* officer
40 Like windows
41 Slamming sites
45 Whopper
46 Mechanical repetition
47 Look, as through a keyhole
50 Large quantities
51 "Average" guy
54 Energy saver
57 Low-___ diet
58 Scrutinize
59 Franciscans, e.g.
60 Purple fruit
61 Makes a 33-Across
62 *"Grazie!"* response

DOWN

1 Off-limits
2 Ceramist's need
3 Lose zip
4 Street shader
5 Author Sendak
6 Serene
7 Goes bad
8 Sculler's need
9 Impertinent
10 *The Cosby Show* daughter
11 Tampers with
12 Contemporary of Agatha
13 Hoe's target
18 Karate school
19 It comes from the heart
23 Road branching
24 Bunches
25 Madrigal group
26 Arledge of the TV Hall of Fame
27 Not seriously
28 During
29 Levels
30 Wasted no time
31 Support group
35 Satiety
36 Rival of Björn
37 Niels Bohr, for one
39 Flight part
40 Break in a race
42 Disco light
43 Stuff in salads
44 Speckled horse
47 Some GIs
48 It offers King David Lounges
49 100 cents, in Spain
50 Emulate Ella
51 Hardy title character
52 Designer Cassini
53 River of Spain
55 Ecol., e.g.
56 Winter comment

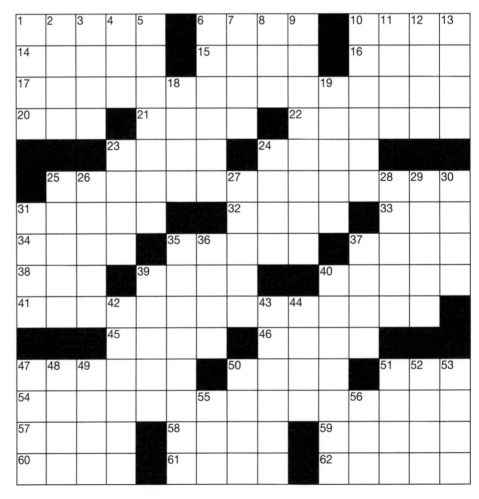

Draw five squares in the diagram so that each corner of each square is on a dot. The squares may be at any angle. Dots may be used for more than one square, or not be used at all.

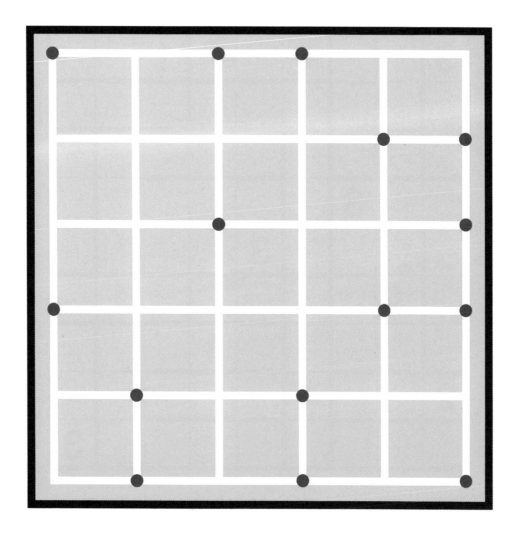

Small Change

Change one letter in each of these two words to form a common two-word phrase. For example, PANTRY CHEW becomes PASTRY CHEF.

PINE CREAM

_____

Fill in the diagram so that each rectangular piece contains the digits 1, 2, and 3 once each, according to these rules: 1) No two horizontally or vertically adjacent squares can contain the same digit. 2) Each completed row and column of the diagram must have an equal number of 1's, 2's, and 3's.

Wrong Is Right

Which of these four words is misspelled?

A) tsunami

B) daquiri

C) cannoli

D) samurai

★★★ Fences

Connect the dots with vertical or horizontal lines so that a single loop is formed with no crossings or branches. Each number indicates how many lines surround it; squares with no number may be surrounded by any number of lines.

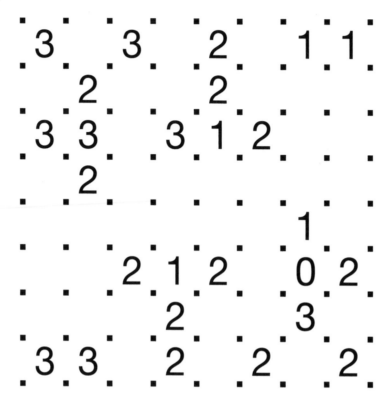

S U D O K U   S U M

Fill in the missing digits from 1 to 9 so that each is used once and the sum of each row and column is as indicated.

Example:

	12	14	19
6			3
17	6		
22		8	

Answer:

	12	14	19
6	1	2	3
17	6	4	7
22	5	8	9

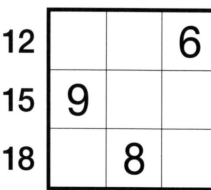

	13	15	17
12			6
15	9		
18		8	

★★★★ Columbus Natives by Stanley Newman

ACROSS

1 Stylish
5 Gardener's need
10 Hemingway nickname
14 Slightly, to Solti
15 Fire stirrer
16 Reunion goer
17 Still not settled
18 Whodunit plot line
19 Destructive hurricane of 2005
20 Golf great from Columbus, Ohio
23 Improper application
26 Betrays fear
27 Opposite of active
28 Likely to spill the beans
32 Raptor or Hawk
33 Expel
34 Erstwhile phone company
37 Author born in Columbus, Georgia
41 Journal VIPs
42 River of Spain
43 Annoy
44 Very beginning
46 In reserve
47 Mini music players
50 Less bumpy
51 Author born in Columbus, Ohio
56 Wordsworth works
57 "... yonder window breaks" speaker
58 Keep ___ on (watch)
62 5th-century invaders
63 Centennial State resort
64 Environs
65 Letters on a Schirra suit
66 Annoying
67 Boomers' successor

DOWN

1 USN junior officer trainer
2 Short trip
3 Chilly cubes
4 Does some spelling?
5 Part of 65-Across
6 Tyler successor
7 Not dissimilar
8 Figure skater Thomas
9 *The Little Mermaid* prince
10 Use as leverage
11 Second name?
12 Built
13 Collect for oneself
21 Toon dog of the future
22 Putin's onetime employer
23 Cut into tiny pieces
24 Needing assistance
25 Former owner of Lands' End
28 Flops on stage
29 Pelf, pejoratively
30 What Brits call a cravat
31 Horsepower fraction
34 Arrive
35 Buying and selling
36 Organic compound
38 Web suffix
39 Brigade's break
40 High-tech team game
44 Ukraine port
45 Destroyer designation
47 New Testament book
48 City west of Venice
49 Foretokens
50 Violin peg material
52 Kisser
53 Gardener's need
54 Tennis officials
55 Unpleasant aroma
59 Live
60 Anne and Jerry's boy
61 Big band instrument

Fill in the blank squares so that every row, column, 3×3 box, *and* each of the 3×3 gray regions contains the digits 1 through 9 exactly once each.

8					3		1	
		2				4		
	6	7			2	5		
		9	5				8	3
		8						4
		6						
				2			6	7
					7		9	1
						2		

MIXAGRAMS

Each line contains a five-letter word and a four-letter word that have been mixed together. (The order of the letters in each word has not been changed.) Unmix the two words on each line and write them in the spaces provided. For example, D A R I U N V E T = DRIVE + AUNT. When you're done, find a two-part answer to the clue by reading down two letter columns in the answers.

CLUE: 2016, for one

L E D G A U T L Y = _ _ _ _ _ + _ _ _ _

E G R A L U S E E = _ _ _ _ _ + _ _ _ _

A P P A L R E T A = _ _ _ _ _ + _ _ _ _

P I U S E T E R Y = _ _ _ _ _ + _ _ _ _

In this crossword puzzle with no clues, each answer consists of two words whose spellings are the same except for the pairs of consecutive letters given. All answers are common words (no phrases), and none are hyphenated or capitalized. Some individual clues may have more than one solution, but only one word pair will correctly link up with all other word pairs.

Transdeletion

Delete one letter from the word UNVEILING and anagram the rest to get something you might order in an Italian restaurant.

_____

ACROSS

1 What you wear
5 Cambridge carriage
9 Bangladesh capital
14 Kona cookout
15 45 player
16 One with a flashlight
17 Thor's dad
18 Folklore monster
19 North Sea feeder
20 Sweetheart workin' in a dairy?
23 Frequent fund-raiser
24 Author Harte
25 Bound
27 Anyone but us
30 German state
33 A deadly sin
34 Big rig
35 Network with a running ticker
37 Dismissive word
38 Dismissive words
41 ___ good deed
42 Works on, as a break
44 Site for roasting
45 RNA and DNA
47 Comeback
49 Schussing spots
50 AMEX alternative
51 Familiar with
52 Manx male
54 Dweeb doin' housework?
60 Japanese dog

62 All fired up
63 Buck heroine
64 Tread neighbor
65 Suffrage
66 Analogy phrase
67 Nuisances
68 Water carrier
69 Retreat

DOWN

1 Steal, so to speak
2 German export
3 Commuter line
4 Barracks installation
5 Calls
6 Appropriate
7 Bushy do
8 Bearing
9 First American auto company
10 Blond shade
11 Pickpocket practicin' golf?
12 Bit of bread
13 Geometric calculation
21 Like some vbs.
22 Rock icon
26 Eyebrow shape
27 Declines, with "out"
28 More loyal
29 Girl usin' her fists?
30 Misrepresent
31 Old Testament book
32 Residence

34 ASAP, in the OR
36 Musical Mama
39 Henry Ford's son
40 Hawk's weapon
43 See suddenly
46 Bring together
48 Nicholson trio
49 Website architect
51 Bring together
52 Diamond cover
53 Tom Joad, for one
55 Roof feature
56 Own up to
57 In addition
58 "Heck!"
59 Bend or hitch
61 Vietnamese holiday

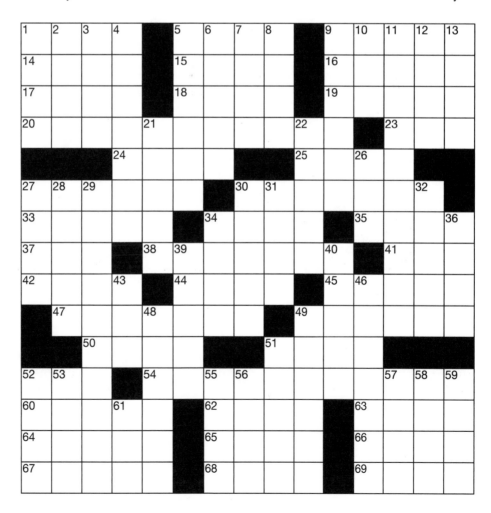

Enter the maze from the left as indicated by the arrow, pass through all the stars exactly once each, then exit at right. You may not retrace your path.

Betweener

What five-letter word can go between the two words below so that it forms compound words with both the word preceding it and the word following it?

WORK __ __ __ __ __ **CRAFT**

Shade squares so that no number appears in any row or column more than once. Shaded squares may not touch each other horizontally or vertically, and all unshaded squares must form a single continuous area.

6	6	5	4	2	1
5	4	2	6	1	3
3	4	6	4	5	4
2	5	6	2	6	4
2	1	4	1	3	4
6	3	3	5	1	2

Think Alike

Unscramble the letters in the phrase CAMEL SNEER to form two words with the same or similar meanings. For example, BEST RATING can be anagrammed to spell START and BEGIN.

_____   _____

The map below represents a set of intersecting streets on which a road rally (starting at A and ending at B) is taking place. The black squares represent checkpoints. You must find a route that starts at A, passes through all checkpoints exactly once, and ends at B. Arrows indicate one-way traffic for that block only. No intersection may be entered more than once.

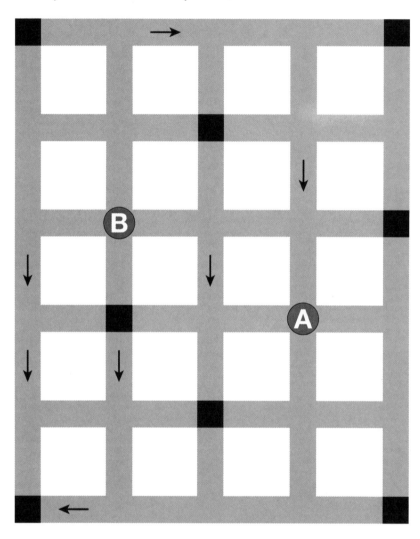

Sound Thinking

There are only two common uncapitalized words whose consonant sounds are V and J, in that order. What are they?

_____   _____

ACROSS

1 Unfortunate
5 Oil container
9 No longer on deck
14 Fully qualified
15 Seep slowly
16 Tabriz native
17 Willie Nelson tune, after 39-Across
19 Aired a second time
20 Rises up
21 Goes off
23 Mare's meal
25 19th Amendment subject
26 Scattering about
30 Chaplin's cane, e.g.
32 Caustic substance
35 Vestige
36 Long baths
37 Part of HMS
38 Size up
39 See 17-Across, 60-Across, 11-Down, and 28-Down
40 Horne of *Cabin in the Sky*
41 Bothered, with "at"
42 Small rows
43 Cleans, as a rug
44 According to
45 Headland
46 Large quantity
47 Cold feet
49 *The Persistence of Memory* artist
51 Mag with an "As They Grow" column
54 "New York, New York" artist
59 Treat with contempt
60 Bad way to start, after 39-Across
62 Golfer with an army
63 Bee or Em

64 Unseat
65 Lugged around
66 Head honcho, perhaps
67 Dental exam ritual

DOWN

1 Henry VIII's VIth
2 Orchestra member
3 Norwegian royal name
4 Word processor command
5 Soldier's ID
6 Prepare, as peanuts
7 Israeli weapon
8 Knit
9 Prepares, as a corn snack
10 Source of enjoyment
11 In advance, after 39-Across
12 Gray's subj.
13 Sardine containers
18 By itself
22 Bring forth
24 Saw
26 Watch attachment
27 Pontificate
28 Brando film, after 39-Across
29 Windshield annoyance
31 Root words
33 Streisand title role
34 Remove
36 Interrupting sound
39 Visual illusion genre
40 MGM mascot
42 Read quickly
43 Sound of a spring
46 Thin pancake
48 Haunting
50 All together
51 H.S. exam
52 It means "height"
53 Pull a switch
55 Crazy like ___
56 Excursion
57 Sub ___ (secretly)
58 Dept. of Justice employee
61 Capek play

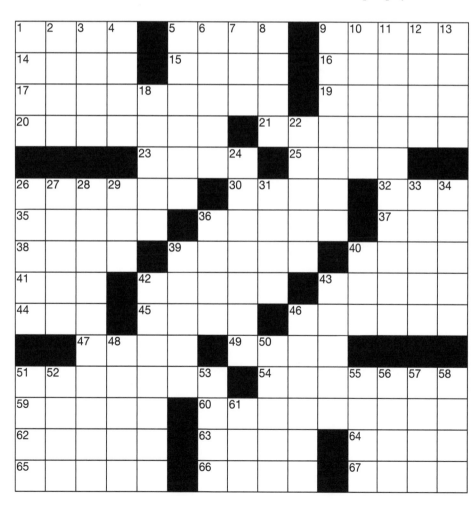

Fill in the blank squares so that every row, column, and 3×3 box contains the digits 1 through 9 exactly once each.

7		3	5		2	8		4
6	8						7	9
	5			7			1	
	4			1			2	
1	9						3	5
8		2	3		4	1		6

M I X A G R A M S

Each line contains a five-letter word and a four-letter word that have been mixed together. (The order of the letters in each word has not been changed.) Unmix the two words on each line and write them in the spaces provided. For example, D A R I U N V E T = DRIVE + AUNT. When you're done, find a multipart answer to the clue by reading down two letter columns in the answers.

CLUE: Fisher tune

R A P I D I T S O = _ _ _ _ _ + _ _ _ _

C R A B U S E T H = _ _ _ _ _ + _ _ _ _

P O S P L A S E M = _ _ _ _ _ + _ _ _ _

S A N G O W E D Y = _ _ _ _ _ + _ _ _ _

★★★ Star Search

Can you find the stars hidden in some of the blank squares? Numbered squares indicate how many stars are hidden in the squares adjacent to them in any direction (including diagonally). There is never more than one star in any square.

1	1	1	1	1	1	1		
2		4					2		1
1			3	5					1
1		2		2			2		1
1									
				2					

C H O I C E   W O R D S

Form three six-letter words from the same category by selecting one letter from each column three times. Each letter will be used exactly once.

Example:　B　A　B　C　O　T　　Answer: BOBCAT, JAGUAR, OCELOT
　　　　　　J　O　E　U　A　R
　　　　　　O　C　G　L　A　T

　　　　　F　U　R　D　O　E　　_ _ _ _ _ _

　　　　　P　O　L　S　O　W　　_ _ _ _ _ _

　　　　　S　H　A　L　U　W　　_ _ _ _ _ _

★★★★ Con Game by Doug Peterson

ACROSS

1 Federal agent
5 Coveted statuette
10 Steals
14 Low-lying region
15 *The Bonfire of the Vanities* author
16 British portraitist
17 With feet turned in
19 Wrangle
20 Knight of song
21 Promised to give up
23 Accidental success
25 Overhead trains
26 Shakespearean rebuke
29 "I Fall to Pieces" singer
34 Expanse
36 Talk big
37 Floppy lid
38 Flew the coop
39 Hoopla
41 Luminesce, in ad-speak
42 Five-star nickname
43 Suffix for ranch
44 Former senator from Maine
46 Blacksmith, at times
48 *Star Wars* star
51 Roddick of tennis
52 "Told ya!"
53 City on the Rhone
55 Reference point
59 Absorb
63 Like crayons
64 Ride-hitching swimmer

66 Lot measurement
67 Studio warning sign
68 *Casablanca* role
69 Warship officer
70 Brine-cured cheeses
71 Legal injury

DOWN

1 Common sitcom rating
2 Correspondence
3 Rootless plant
4 Required
5 Confesses
6 W.C. Fields persona
7 Approximately
8 Not many
9 Make over
10 Onetime *Monday Night Football* regular
11 The other side
12 "La Vie en Rose" singer
13 Feudal worker
18 Thimble Theatre surname
22 Odd-numbered pages
24 Big bang
26 Violinist Zimbalist
27 Jeweled headpiece
28 Jazz instruments
30 With wisdom
31 Couture monogram
32 Unfurnished

33 Nail smoother
35 Made tracks
40 High-tech ID
45 University of Arizona athlete
47 Loses one's cool
49 Nairobi native
50 Hapless ones
54 Swe. neighbor
55 Tar's mop
56 Poi base
57 Since
58 Old Norse character
60 Metric prefix
61 Cold War power
62 Super
65 Imported auto

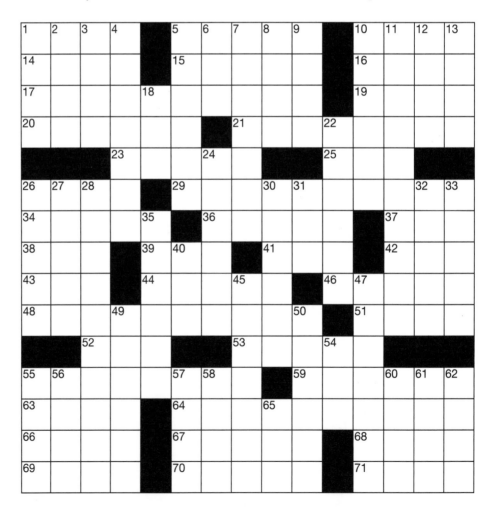

Enter the maze, pass through all the yellow circles exactly once, then exit by the shortest possible path. You must go with the flow of the road, making no sharp turns. You may use paths more than once.

Say It Again

What five-letter word can be either a feature of wood or something grown on a farm?

__ __ __ __ __

Enter the letters A, B, and C into the diagram, filling in some (but not all) of the squares so that each row and column contains each letter exactly once. The letters outside the diagram indicate the first letter encountered in the indicated row or column when moving in the direction of the arrow from that side of the grid.

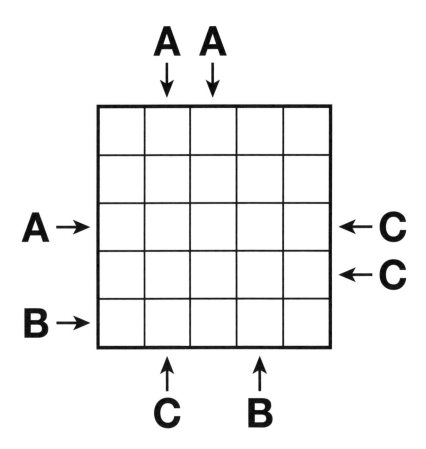

Two-by-Four

The eight letters in the word HENHOUSE can be rearranged in only one way to form a pair of common, unhyphenated four-letter words. Can you find them?

___ ___ ___ ___   ___ ___ ___ ___

ACROSS

1 Two at a time
7 Product once endorsed by Joe DiMaggio
15 How some may be awakened
16 Principally
17 Keyless
18 Shut up
19 "The Song Is ___" (Kern tune)
20 Doesn't keep up
22 Good source of vitamin A
23 Moves back
25 George Gordon ___ Byron
27 Two-time U.S. Open champ
28 One number
30 Darwin greeting
32 Fissure
33 Monopoly token
35 100 pounds of nails
37 One way to order eggs
38 Feature of some knitted hats
43 Wasn't used
44 Clinton cabinet member
45 Recess with a vault
49 Ben's girlfriend in *Meet the Parents*
51 University of California campus
52 Have no perceptible separation
54 Cherry et al.
56 Flutters
57 Erstwhile game show mogul
59 Duty
61 Area of responsibility, so to speak
62 Directly

64 Filmdom's Major Frank Burns
66 Pretty cool
67 Hematology concern
68 Wheel holders
69 Amount cashed, at times

DOWN

1 Beseeched
2 Cologne debut of 1931
3 Remark of the unsold
4 Nickelodeon toon
5 It first flew in 1948
6 Kennedy Center honoree of 1997
7 Came together
8 Box score column heading
9 Legendary Celtic king
10 Dutch ___
11 What Brits call a "wing"
12 Easy
13 Natural roll
14 First to arrive
21 Dynamo
24 Yokozuna's specialty
26 Spot for a cabin
29 Columbia offerings
31 Shout of approval
34 It has "arguments" and "logic games" sections
36 Erstwhile Lenin follower

39 Mr. Olympia's lack
40 Icon of the Sixties
41 It first flew in 1947
42 Bomb, for one
45 Brothers' bosses
46 Source of energy, in astrology
47 Composed
48 Dress
50 Extends
53 Type of car
55 Type of car
58 Golf club part
60 It's a shore thing
63 Likewise not
65 Appraise for authenticity

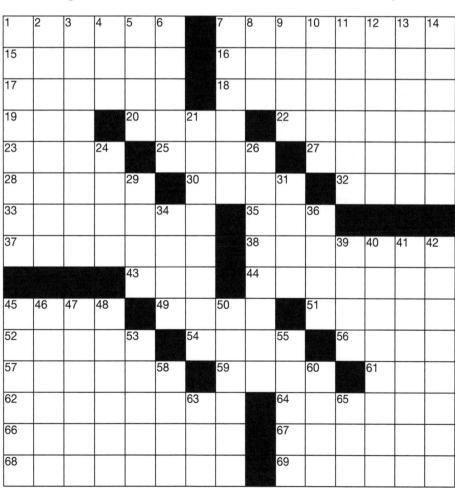

Ten ships of four different sizes (shown below left) are hidden in the diagram. Ships may be oriented horizontally or vertically, and may not touch each other, not even diagonally. A square containing wavy lines represents open water; such a square will not contain any part of a ship. Numbers at the edge of the diagram indicate how many squares in that row or column contain parts of ships, including any which may have already been placed as clues.

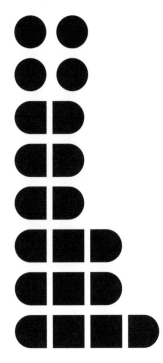

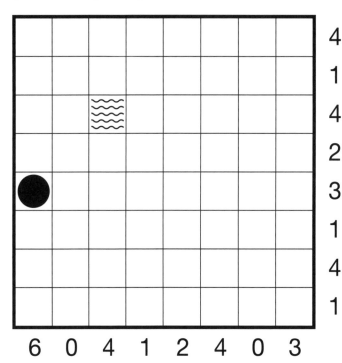

CLUELESS CROSSWORD

Complete the crossword with common, uncapitalized seven-letter words, based on the letters already filled in for you.

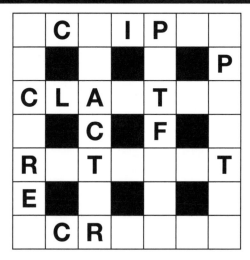

Fill in the blank squares so that every row, column, 3×3 box, *and* each of the 3×3 gray regions contains the digits 1 through 9 exactly once each.

6					7			
7	4				3			6
	9		8			1		
				1	9			8
							1	
3					2			7
1								
		8	5					
						2		

Who's What Where?

The correct term for a resident of the African nation of Zimbabwe is:

A) Zimbabwean

B) Zimbabwite

C) Zimbabian

D) Babwaka

Betweener

What six-letter word can go between the two words below so that it forms compound words with both the word preceding it and the word following it?

BAR __ __ __ __ __ __ **FOOT**

★★★★★ Themeless Toughie by Daniel R. Stark

ACROSS

1 Second-story man
8 Fresco bases
15 Narrow, in a way
16 Item
17 Plum relative
18 Less arid
19 Flat-tasting
20 Ebbets Field great
22 Gladiator's greeting
23 Is off one's feed
24 Fly catchers
25 *Bonjour Tristesse* author
27 Certain runner
28 *Julius Caesar* setting
30 Pick a ticket
31 Pantry accessory
33 It rises in the Swiss Alps
35 Units of energy
36 Longtime *New Yorker* critic
37 Arm bones
39 Keeps in thrall
43 Peeved
44 Prize
46 Stopping place
47 Mountain people
49 Versatile vehicles
50 Salmon variety
51 ___ disadvantage
52 Duct
54 Good for grinding
55 Destroyers, so to speak
57 Lofty
59 Sporting warning
60 Court
61 Most mysterious
62 Like some paper goods

DOWN

1 Pretentious talk
2 Different
3 Royal emblems
4 Secluded spots
5 Capture
6 Crumb toter
7 Rams, perhaps
8 Having the most grit
9 Piccadilly statue
10 Filthy places
11 Mama's girl
12 1080-degree figure
13 Heighten
14 Royal epithet
21 It began as AuctionWeb in 1995
24 Shoe style
26 Walled Spanish city
28 Draped dress
29 Tapes over
32 Gave up
34 Position of authority
36 Pew adjuncts
37 Unremarkable
38 Set up
39 Friend of Wonder Woman
40 Raging
41 Heighten
42 Expressed indignation
43 Copied Kwan
45 Last stage
48 Induce to jump
50 Literary middle name
53 Added stipulations
54 Save one's speech
56 Keep from increasing
58 Soft footwear

Connect the dots with vertical or horizontal lines so that a single loop is formed with no crossings or branches. Each number indicates how many lines surround it; squares with no number may be surrounded by any number of lines.

```
2 3         0   3

  3     1 3

          3             3

    2 1     3

          2     2 3

  3             1

          2 1         2

  3   2           2 1
```

In Other Words

There is only one common uncapitalized word that contains the consecutive sequence of letters YGN. What is the word?

_____

Think Alike

Unscramble the letters in the phrase NEW BOULDER to form two words with the same or similar meanings. For example, BEST RATING can be anagrammed to spell START and BEGIN.

_____   _____

★★★★★ Themeless Toughie by Merle Baker

ACROSS

1 Tricks
6 Standard paragraphs
11 Doddering
12 Approaches maturity
14 Comment at length
15 Across the ocean
17 Tributes
18 Impedes
19 Turns up
20 Desktop device
21 Third party of 1848
23 Most-produced organic compound
24 Siesta time
25 Weighed down
27 Sale items, at times
28 Estimation
33 Dumbfounded
38 Soft touch
39 Lizards' lodgings, perhaps
41 Martian features
43 Aerialist action
44 Don't mind
45 *World News Tonight* creator
46 Webs
47 More outdated
48 Senior
49 Folds
50 *American Dreams* actor
51 Bluish gray

DOWN

1 Hero
2 Having no zip
3 Closely connected
4 Climate phenomenon
5 Reserves
6 Puts pressure on
7 Construction crew
8 Do business
9 Symbols of innocence
10 Stores in the country
11 *Evita* title
13 Greek moon goddess
14 Ceramic center
16 With 32-Down, flush
22 *American Graffiti* star
26 1960s decor items
27 Scatter
28 Lab assortment
29 Double Oscar nominee of 1993
30 Early deal
31 Almanac entries
32 See 16-Down
33 Water split in 1987
34 Regards with wonderment
35 Dryness
36 Burns, in a way
37 EMT accessory
40 Cube do-over
42 IT setups

Fill in the diagram so that each rectangular piece contains the digits 1, 2, and 3 once each, according to these rules: 1) No two horizontally or vertically adjacent squares can contain the same digit.
2) Each completed row and column of the diagram must have an equal number of 1's, 2's, and 3's.

ADDITION SWITCH

Switch the positions of two digits in the incorrect sum at right to get a correct sum. For example, in the incorrect sum 955 + 264 = 411, you would swap the second 1 in 411 with the 9 in 955 to get the correct sum 155 + 264 = 419.

```
  559
+428
-----
  785
```

★★★ Number-Out

Shade squares so that no number appears in any row or column more than once. Shaded squares may not touch each other horizontally or vertically, and all unshaded squares must form a single continuous area.

5	3	1	1	4	6
3	6	1	4	6	6
2	1	1	5	6	3
1	5	6	4	2	1
4	2	2	3	5	1
4	4	5	4	1	3

Wrong Is Right

Which of these four words is misspelled?

A) boutonniere

B) bouillon

C) bouillabaise

D) bourgeois

Small Change

Change one letter in each of these two words to form a common two-word phrase. For example, PANTRY CHEW becomes PASTRY CHEF.

CORD FLAMES

_____

ACROSS

1 Perfume essences
7 Works on walls
15 Nonsense
16 Test taker
17 Berth place
18 Weigh heavily
19 *The Unanswered Question* composer
20 Sings lustily
22 Relief preceder
23 Phone book abbr.
24 Annoy
25 Champagne bottle
27 Island farewell
29 Miami-___ County
31 Late-night alumnus
32 Furniture polish ingredient
34 Elf-sized
36 Hinge (on)
37 Baja souvenir
40 Ames inst.
41 Manhandling
43 Toaster ___
46 Fish dish
48 Rice-A-Roni corporate colleague
49 Air pair
51 Skilled
53 Sort of extension
54 Land where Cain lived

55 Damages to reputation
57 Spill it
58 Qualified
60 Check in
62 Unrealistic ideas
63 Car lot convenience
64 Six-time Super Bowl champs
65 Retiring

DOWN

1 Flag rank
2 Went
3 Annoying
4 Bird of ancient Rome
5 Cartoon Chihuahua
6 Writing surface
7 Ouster
8 Away unwillingly
9 Dark shadow
10 Off
11 Theater area
12 Permit
13 Keep in mind
14 Deals with
21 Fixed up
24 Sheets in frames
26 Kindly
28 Optimistic
30 Flock members
33 Difficult task
35 Blow
37 Allied

38 Supply route
39 Shackles
41 Folly
42 Savoy Opera collaborator
43 ___ manual
44 Illinois state flower
45 Salad green
47 Trucking company
50 Frosting effect
52 Literally, "song sung to a harp"
56 1996 award for *Rent*
57 George's nickname for Omar
59 Thou
61 Boomer or doe

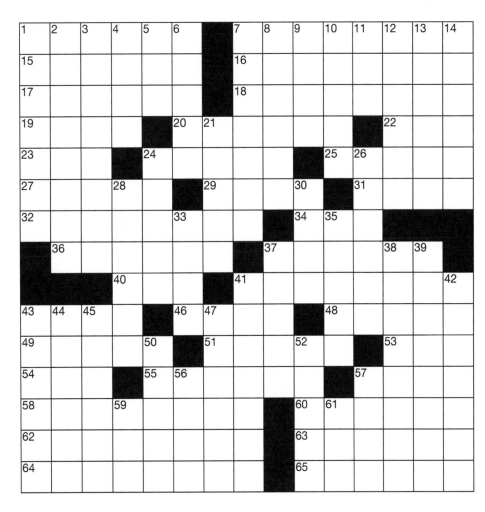

★★★ Color Paths

Find the shortest path through the maze from the entrance at the bottom to the center, by using the colored paths in this sequence: red, blue, yellow, red, blue, yellow, etc. When you reach a white square, you must continue on a path of the next color in the sequence. You may retrace your path.

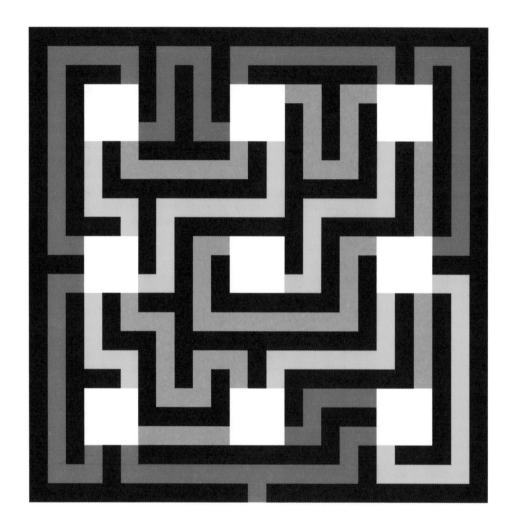

Say It Again

What six-letter word can be either someone playing a certain sport or a type of hat?

___ ___ ___ ___ ___ ___

ACROSS

1 Clear drifts
5 Calligraphy tool
10 Spy tools, for short
14 Spiel
15 "New Deal for Christmas" musical
16 *Tess of the D'Urbervilles* scoundrel
17 *London Fields* author
18 Legendary lamenter
19 Endure successfully, with "out"
20 Something to pitch
21 Raft
22 Cant
24 Blissful
26 Social ___
27 Some demonstrations
28 Oscar-winning Washington film
29 Oath of old
30 Lack of conviction
31 Patterned after
34 Paper holder
37 Most letters, in D.C.
38 Soapy sales
39 Surfer's need
40 Crack
41 Boston suburb
42 Ancient document
45 Started gently
46 Discernment
47 W. Sahara neighbor
48 *WKRP* name
49 Check
50 Allen role
52 Teri, in *Young Frankenstein*
53 String ensemble
54 Act unprofessionally
55 *South Park* kid
56 O.T. prophet
57 Played an old instrument
58 Squirts

DOWN

1 Certain cell fragments
2 Diva's spot
3 Up there
4 Shark territory
5 World's oldest independent airline
6 It may have many locals
7 Apprised of
8 Ad follower
9 Broadway's first Willy Loman
10 Riddler portrayer
11 Justify
12 French wine region
13 Part of a trailer
23 *TV Guide* data
25 Risky
26 Funny money
28 Lost cause
30 Big blockers
31 Expanded
32 Making uncomfortable, perhaps
33 Ones from Yerevan
35 Long-locked character
36 King or Queen
40 Equation element
41 Irregular
42 Covenants
43 Auto debut of 1986
44 Fast of Esther follower
45 Tony group
47 Like crazy
51 Six-foot-tall trotter

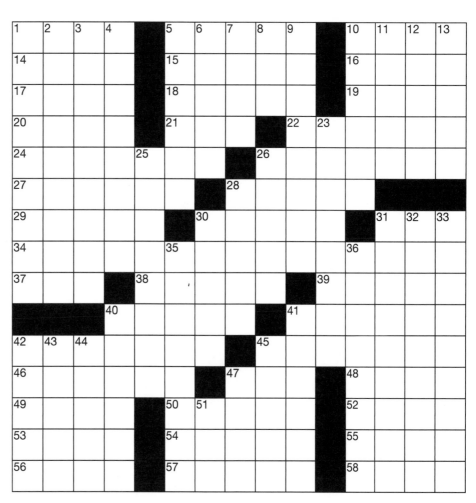

Enter the letters A, B, C, and D into the diagram, filling in some (but not all) of the squares so that each row and column contains each letter exactly once. The letters outside the diagram indicate the first letter encountered in the indicated row or column when moving in the direction of the arrow from that side of the grid.

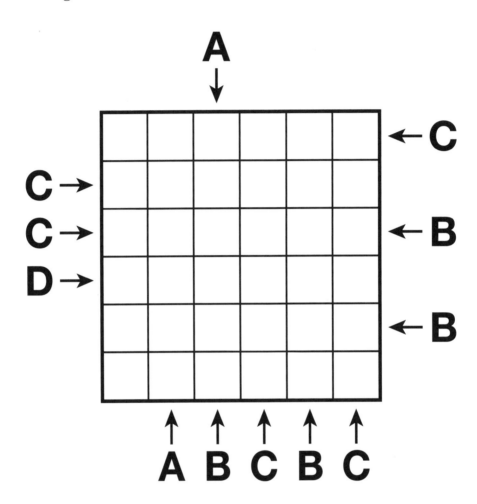

National Treasure

The words INGROWN and NEARING can each be formed by anagramming seven of the nine letters in what European language?

__ __ __ __ __ __ __ __ __

★★★★ Sudoku

Fill in the blank squares so that every row, column, and 3×3 box contains the digits 1 through 9 exactly once each.

	1				3			
5		2					8	
		1		3				
	3					1	4	
		5		8				
7	4				6			
		6		4				
9				7			1	
	8				9			

M I X A G R A M S

Each line contains a five-letter word and a four-letter word that have been mixed together. (The order of the letters in each word has not been changed.) Unmix the two words on each line and write them in the spaces provided. For example, D A R I U N V E T = DRIVE + AUNT. When you're done, find a two-part answer to the clue by reading down two letter columns in the answers.

CLUE: Canine command

T O R N O L L U S = _ _ _ _ _ + _ _ _ _

V E T O A S A L T = _ _ _ _ _ + _ _ _ _

E L D G L E A M A = _ _ _ _ _ + _ _ _ _

R U G L O N G A T = _ _ _ _ _ + _ _ _ _

★★★★★ Themeless Toughie by Anna Stiga

ACROSS

1 Big rattle
7 Sort of soup
13 *Star Trek* villain
14 Mistaken
16 Making up
17 Patriarch of an artistic family
18 Tried to open
19 Calzone center
20 It's no biggie
21 Refrain sound
22 Fire ___
24 Ate
25 Something called
27 Agency
30 Wonder
31 Creator name
33 Dangerous proteins
35 Check phrasing
40 Quizzical comment
41 Obdurate
42 Popular space-saving device
45 Like clay
47 No longer skeptical
48 Pictures of health
50 Purposes
52 No, to Bond
53 Prevailing style
54 Porridge tidbit
56 Tar
58 Picks
60 Spanish rice ingredient
61 Treat like a VIP
62 Courtroom verb
63 Big bills
64 Word from the Icelandic for "gush"

DOWN

1 Name first used for car radios
2 Without regard for values
3 Archaeological inscription
4 Kirk Douglas, for one
5 Harvard student
6 Emma's director for *Sense and Sensibility*
7 See 15-Down
8 Not currently
9 Unfamiliar
10 "Shoot!"
11 Heinz brand
12 Procrastinator's plaint
13 Difficult situation
15 With 7-Down, dry drink
19 Put back, in a way
23 Three-time Hackman role
24 Cash
26 Plaster backing
28 Mass departure
29 Bearing
32 Ball game, informally
34 Arranges carefully
36 Not a lot
37 Auto designer's concern
38 Witness
39 ___ case
42 Glorify
43 Torrid Zone boundary
44 Field of stars on the U.S. flag
46 Oil source
49 Kind of question
51 Witless
54 Exude slowly
55 Athena's half-brother
57 Broker's offerings
59 Qualified
60 Chinese zodiac beast

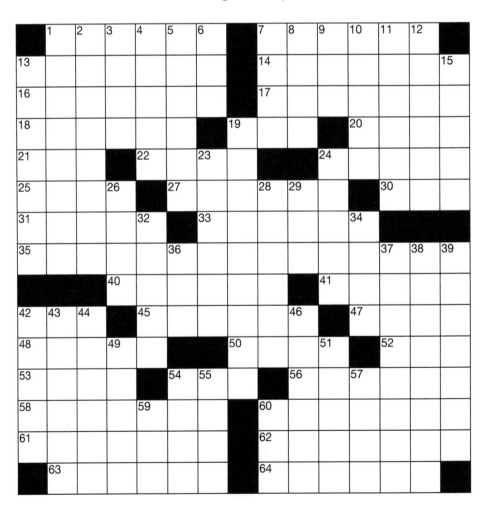

★★★★ One-Way Streets

The map below represents a set of intersecting streets on which a road rally is taking place. The black squares represent checkpoints. The S's stand for "start" and "stop," but which is which is left for you to determine. You must find a route that starts at one S, passes through all checkpoints exactly once, and ends at the other S. Arrows indicate one-way traffic for that block only. No intersection may be entered more than once.

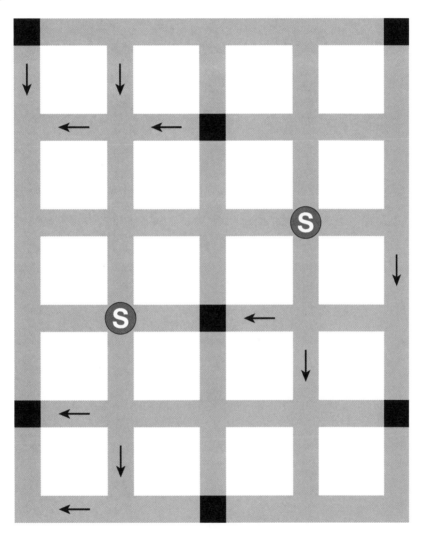

★★ Split Decisions

In this crossword puzzle with no clues, each answer consists of two words whose spellings are the same except for the pairs of consecutive letters given. All answers are common words (no phrases), and none are hyphenated or capitalized. Some individual clues may have more than one solution, but only one word pair will correctly link up with all other word pairs.

Transdeletion

Delete one letter from the word CYNOPHILE (which means "a dog lover") and anagram the rest to get a game.

_____

ACROSS

1 Outgoing
7 Demographic categories
14 Grow gradually
15 Shout of joy
16 Dark blue grape
17 Hobbyist's activity
18 Bobble something
19 Like serge
21 Middle Ages literary figure
22 Blocks
24 Is complicit in
26 Japanese delicacy
27 Current event
28 Mark of Zorro
29 Dust devil
30 Honorary title
32 Red-headed doll
34 It's left
35 Loving
39 Body of *eau*
40 Not fit to gobble
41 Doesn't keep up
44 Tilts
46 Bit of help
47 Capital of Laos
48 On the decline
49 1960s PBS host
50 Disconcert
52 Summer music
54 Schmooze
55 Some camera apertures
57 Go up
59 Lazy
60 Ended one's resistance
61 "Piece of cake!"
62 Stable population

DOWN

1 Course length
2 Eventually
3 Eats up
4 Hostile
5 Confesses
6 Apollo's mother
7 High-tech replicas
8 Outmoded
9 Doesn't ignore
10 Piece of earthenware
11 Bankrupt
12 ___ glass
13 As Solomon would
15 Ones with pseudopods
20 Hold dear
23 Insurance contract word
25 Punting site
28 Plaster product
29 Lard
31 Operetta princess
33 One way to agree
35 First stakes
36 Commit
37 Lamented loudly
38 Nursery features
40 Be firm
41 Be rash
42 White elephant, for one
43 Secretive group
45 Fiery
48 Sound
49 Wish for
51 Present
53 Simple teeth, perhaps
56 Green land
58 Project conclusion

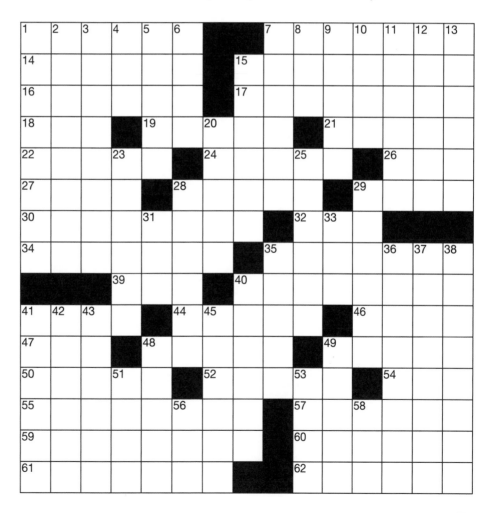

★★★★ Turn Maze

Entering the maze at the bottom and exiting at the top (without accidentally going through the other exits), find the shortest past through the maze following these rules: You must turn right on red squares, turn left on blue squares, and go straight through yellow squares. Your path may retrace itself and cross itself at intersections, but you may not make U-turns.

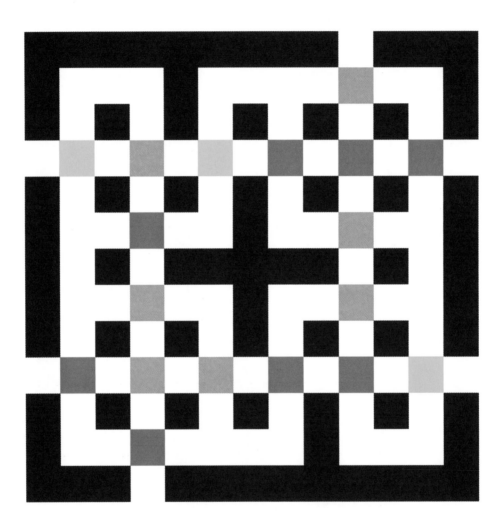

Say It Again

What six-letter word can be either a part of some garments or a verb meaning "arrest"?

—— —— —— —— —— ——

Can you find the stars hidden in some of the blank squares? Numbered squares indicate how many stars are hidden in the squares adjacent to them in any direction (including diagonally). There is never more than one star in any square.

	4		2		2	
2						
	3		2		3	
2						2
	4		5			
2					1	2
	2		2	3		
						3
	1	1		2		1

CHOICE WORDS

Form three six-letter words from the same category by selecting one letter from each column three times. Each letter will be used exactly once.

Example: B A B C O T   Answer: BOBCAT, JAGUAR, OCELOT
          J O E U A R
          O C G L A T

C L I N R L   _ _ _ _ _ _

P H E E E H   _ _ _ _ _ _

W R I S C S   _ _ _ _ _ _

★★★★★ Themeless Toughie by Doug Peterson

ACROSS

1 Basis for a WWII code
7 Outfield area
13 *The End of Eternity* author
14 Clambake items
16 Gliding dance step
17 They're in some jams
18 *In the Meadow* artist
19 Most like a beanpole
20 Intention
21 Film role portrayed by Skippy
23 *On the Road* narrator
24 Shells
26 Small prop
29 Tiger's turf
32 Scotch water
33 Spanish island
35 Got more serious
38 Light on a set
39 Impertinent look
40 Waterford's home
41 Runner of a sort
42 Comparatively cool
45 How to address a maj. gen.?
46 River of Yakutsk
47 Free-bird filler
50 Comfort food
54 Sparing
56 Fascinate
57 Sign on
58 Ride roughshod over
59 Fictional taskmaster
60 Dripping, in a way
61 Soothing

DOWN

1 Shell liner
2 Far from flush
3 Choice dish
4 Juvenile retort
5 Spode or Wedgwood
6 Technical analysis term
7 Mother with a Nobel Prize
8 Plugging away
9 Box contents
10 ___ pool
11 Fine things
12 Wordless summons
14 One without a handicap
15 Digital watch abbr.
22 Tastelessly overdone
24 MS accompaniment
25 Mothball
26 Carved talisman
27 First name in Israeli politics
28 Unaffectedness
29 Shelters
30 Eminent epidemiologist
31 Four on some faces
34 *Cinderella Man* character
36 Purple shade
37 Premiere of 1989
43 Film actor in nine decades
44 Employee
45 Heart's parts
47 Ancient marketplace
48 Willamette University site
49 Back ___
50 OTC purchases
51 Ample, old-style
52 "You lookin' ___?"
53 Phenomenal flyer
55 Internal motivation

Shade squares so that no number appears in any row or column more than once. Shaded squares may not touch each other horizontally or vertically, and all unshaded squares must form a single continuous area.

2	4	5	1	6	4
4	2	2	6	2	3
5	2	3	2	4	1
4	5	6	3	3	2
3	2	1	5	5	2
4	1	2	4	5	6

Think Alike

Unscramble the letters in the phrase HEAR WOLVES to form two words with the same or similar meanings. For example, BEST RATING can be anagrammed to spell START and BEGIN.

_____   _____

★★★ Line Drawing

Draw three straight lines from edge to edge to make four regions in which words can be formed such that there are two, three, four, and eleven in the four regions.

Two-by-Four

The eight letters in the word IDENTIFY can be rearranged in two different ways to form a pair of common four-letter words. Can you find both pairs?

__ __ __ __   __ __ __ __

__ __ __ __   __ __ __ __

ACROSS

1 Howler
8 Comebacks
15 Let out, maybe
16 Kind of coif
17 Went downhill
18 Band's bar
19 Personal
20 British theatre award
22 Jag accessory
23 More accommodating
25 Geological periods
26 Alligator ___
27 Jeans specification
28 This, to Tomás
29 "Pearl of the South" city
30 Wool source
32 Backed
34 Auto last made in 1957
36 Not relaxed
37 Gone
41 *Survivor* group
44 Cheer
45 Lacking culture
47 Jargon
49 Phi ___ (honor society member)
50 Self ender
51 Under, to Umberto
52 Geological period
53 British dramatist/ lyricist
55 Bucks, for instance
56 Corresponded
58 Excuses
60 Blow up
61 Scholarly
62 Stored, as chestnuts
63 Bugged

DOWN

1 Fraternal group
2 Rancor
3 Letter writer's aid
4 Jane ex
5 Warmth
6 Upset, with "over"
7 Countercurrents
8 Camel or giraffe
9 Weapons with guards
10 Boris Godunov, for one
11 Sounds of discomfort
12 Corned beef sandwiches
13 Apartment amenity
14 Hunted like a caveman
21 Franchise
24 Issue forth
26 Capitol feature
28 Sun spot, sometimes
29 Stream
31 ___ Tranquillitatis
33 See
35 Ushered in
37 Hashes over
38 Refined
39 Literally, "little pan"
40 Waiter's intro
42 Aromatherapy purchase
43 Rapprochement
46 Dredge, perhaps
48 Did a chef's task
50 Resistance reducer
51 Swagger
53 Miss
54 Unusually great
57 Place for slides
59 Carson subject

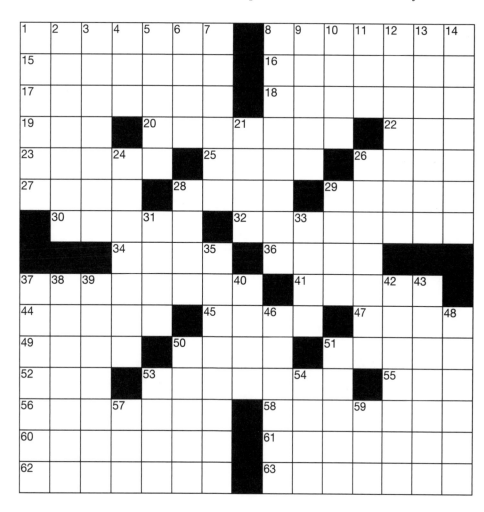

In this crossword puzzle with no clues, each answer consists of two words whose spellings are the same except for the sets of three consecutive letters given. All answers are common words (no phrases), and none are hyphenated or capitalized. Some individual clues may have more than one solution, but only one word pair will correctly link up with all other word pairs.

Delete one letter from the word PROVENANCE and anagram the rest to get a two-word phrase for something found in a kitchen.

_____

★★★ Piece It Together

Fill in the design of blue squares using pieces of the shape outlined in black. The pieces may be rotated or reflected (or both) from the orientation shown.

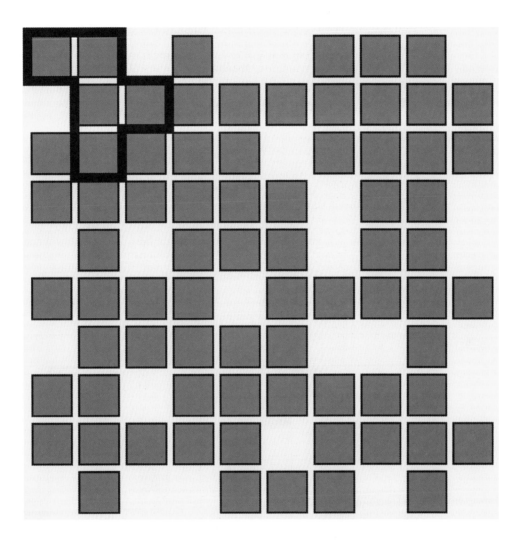

Small Change

Change one letter in each of these two words to form a common two-word phrase. For example, PANTRY CHEW becomes PASTRY CHEF.

TRAY MASTER

_____

ACROSS

1 Whiskas alternative
8 Mastery
15 Book with only one chapter
16 Strike, in a way
17 Unsophisticated quality
18 Seemingly forever
19 Adverse
20 Taft's vice president
22 Under the ___
23 Bun, for one
25 Held, as a trailer
26 Complete rejection
27 Two of Henry VIII's six
29 Didn't act
30 *The Pawnbroker* director
31 Defense program
33 Certain pigeons
34 Historic spot in Surrey
36 One way to cook
39 Klee colleague
43 Outfox
44 Perfectly
45 Song associated with Detroit
46 Name from the Latin for "small"
47 ___ Speaker (contemporary title)
49 Nonspeaking role in *Parsifal*

50 Cooperstown inductee of 1951
51 Single, for one
53 Coll. units
54 Gave up
56 Head of state since 1989
58 Streaming
59 Any of the Magi
60 Biomass product
61 Atomic rearrangements

DOWN

1 Like Elizabethan collars
2 Chinese delicacy
3 Close behind
4 Multiple of CXXXV
5 Moves it
6 Promising words
7 Brings by cart
8 Help out on a line
9 Charged
10 Gulf War ally
11 Overcome adversity
12 Late stages
13 Comparatively bold
14 cummings creations
21 Not to order
24 Trepid
26 Rotator cuff neighbor
28 Crass sound
30 Abundant supplies

32 At all
33 Spell
35 Garbo role of 1931
36 Indiscreet arguers
37 Garry's longtime rival
38 Toon hero of a 2001 film
40 Recent arrival
41 Less dowdy
42 Some muscles
44 Crayon kin
47 Pug's complaint
48 Game show gear
51 Honey
52 VCR descendant
55 Conservation org.
57 Avoid committing

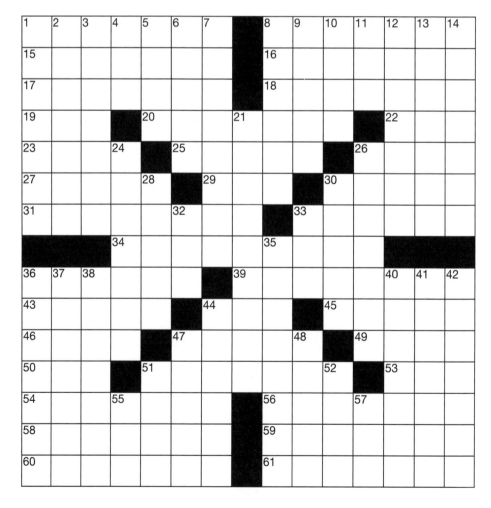

Silent Signals

S	T	A	G	■	L	A	S	S	O	■	S	C	A	M
A	U	T	O	■	O	R	I	O	N	■	E	A	S	E
I	N	T	O	■	W	E	L	L	S	■	E	T	T	E
L	A	N	D	O	F	N	O	D	■	A	S	C	O	T
■	■	B	O	A	T	S	■	S	H	A	H	■	■	■
■	E	G	Y	P	T	■	S	E	A	W	A	L	L	■
H	A	R	E	S	■	T	H	U	M	B	■	W	E	E
E	T	A	■	H	E	I	D	I	■	■	I	N	N	■
M	U	D	■	M	E	L	T	S	■	B	A	N	D	S
S	P	E	C	I	A	L	■	Y	A	N	K	S	■	■
■	P	A	S	T	■	V	I	E	W	S	■	■	■	■
A	B	O	U	T	■	T	I	D	A	L	W	A	V	E
L	E	I	S	■	P	O	S	E	R	■	E	V	I	L
D	A	N	E	■	T	R	I	A	L	■	R	O	S	E
A	R	T	S	■	A	N	T	S	Y	■	S	W	A	M

Falling Leaves

Century Marks
22, 40, 18, 20

Sudoku

2	3	5	6	8	4	1	9	7
4	7	6	9	1	3	5	2	8
1	9	8	5	7	2	3	6	4
6	8	9	1	3	7	2	4	5
7	1	4	2	5	6	8	3	9
5	2	3	8	4	9	7	1	6
8	4	2	7	9	1	6	5	3
3	5	1	4	6	8	9	7	2
9	6	7	3	2	5	4	8	1

Mixagrams

A H E A D   T W I N
L A U G H   J O T S
A R M O R   F O R E
I D E A L   O D D S

Animal Acts

S	A	W	S	■	S	S	T	S	■	L	A	D	L	E
E	T	A	T	■	C	O	A	T	■	I	N	O	I	L
E	L	L	A	■	A	N	T	E	■	B	A	G	E	L
Y	A	K	K	I	N	G	A	W	A	Y	■	G	U	S
A	S	S	E	N	T	■	■	M	A	G	I	■	■	■
■	■	D	Y	N	A	M	O	■	O	N	T	O	■	■
R	A	B	B	I	■	O	W	E	S	■	A	G	I	N
O	P	E	R	A	■	T	A	N	■	S	P	I	L	L
B	E	A	U	■	T	O	I	L	■	P	E	T	T	Y
E	R	R	S	■	O	N	T	O	U	R	■	■	■	■
■	■	I	H	A	D	■	■	S	I	E	S	T	A	■
Y	E	N	■	W	O	L	F	I	N	G	D	O	W	N
M	A	G	N	A	■	A	I	D	E	■	A	R	I	D
C	R	O	O	K	■	G	R	E	W	■	M	T	G	E
A	N	N	I	E	■	S	E	A	S	■	S	A	S	S

Fences

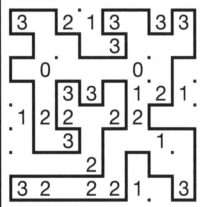

Initial Reaction
Forewarned is forearmed.

Wrong Is Right
B) pervey (should be *purvey*)

Line Drawing

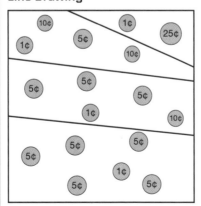

Three of a Kind
We eagerly re**mini**sced about the old La**tin y**ears (wee, mini, tiny).

Who's What Where?
B) Oaklander

Back to School

P	E	S	T	■	S	P	A	S	■	O	H	A	R	A
A	R	E	A	■	L	O	F	T	■	R	I	S	E	S
D	I	E	T	■	O	L	A	Y	■	A	L	I	B	I
S	E	N	T	■	W	O	R	L	D	C	L	A	S	S
■	■	O	W	L	■	■	E	E	L	■	■	■	■	■
P	A	N	O	R	A	M	A	■	W	E	N	T	B	Y
E	M	U	■	E	N	A	C	T	■	■	O	R	E	O
D	I	D	O	N	E	S	H	O	M	E	W	O	R	K
A	G	E	D	■	S	O	F	A	S	■	T	E	E	■
L	O	S	E	R	S	■	O	U	T	P	O	S	T	S
■	■	■	E	A	T	■	■	T	N	T	■	■	■	■
S	T	E	E	P	G	R	A	D	E	■	T	A	P	S
A	O	R	T	A	■	A	M	E	R	■	A	L	O	E
M	E	A	T	Y	■	P	O	L	E	■	W	E	S	T
E	S	S	E	S	■	S	K	I	D	■	A	X	E	S

Number-Out

Think Alike
Yes, okay

In Other Words
Bazaar

Page 18

Five Squares

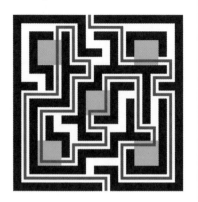

Small Change

Show biz

Page 19

Four Quarters

Page 20

One-Way Streets

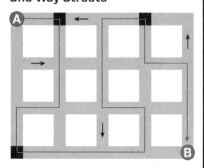

Sound Thinking

Ammonia

Page 21

Split Decisions

Transdeletion

Tense

Page 22

Star Search

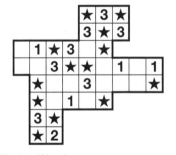

Choice Words

Stymie, thwart, outwit

Page 23

Serve and Protect

C	H	A	P		C	A	C	H	E		A	M	I	D
L	O	B	E		A	L	I	A	S		S	I	D	E
I	B	E	T		D	I	G	I	T		K	N	E	W
P	O	L	I	C	E	C	A	R			T	O	D	A	Y
		T	A	T	E	R		S	O	U	R			
L	O	W	E	R	S			H	O	S	T	E	S	S
E	R	A	S	E		H	A	U	L	S		A	C	T
V	A	T		W	E	D	G	E			D	O	E	
E	T	C		G	R	A	S	S		S	C	E	N	E
R	E	H	I	R	E	D			S	H	A	R	E	D
	S	C	A	N		A	F	T	E	R				
D	A	T	E	D		G	U	A	R	D	R	A	I	L
A	U	R	A		F	E	N	C	E		O	S	L	O
S	T	A	G		A	N	T	E	S		T	I	L	T
H	O	P	E		N	E	S	T	S		S	A	S	S

Page 24

Hyper-Sudoku

8	1	7	9	3	4	2	5	6
2	9	4	6	8	5	3	7	1
6	5	3	2	7	1	9	8	4
3	7	1	8	5	2	6	4	9
5	4	8	3	9	6	7	1	2
9	2	6	4	1	7	5	3	8
7	3	9	1	2	8	4	6	5
4	8	5	7	6	9	1	2	3
1	6	2	5	4	3	8	9	7

Mixagrams

C A B I N	P A C E
S T E R N	F A U N
E X A C T	S P R Y
G O N E R	A D D S

Page 25

123

2	3	1	3	2	1
3	1	2	1	3	2
1	2	3	2	1	3
3	1	2	1	3	2
2	3	1	3	2	1
1	2	3	2	1	3

Sudoku Sum

	15	12	18
18	6	3	9
8	2	1	5
19	7	8	4

Housework

P	A	I	N		A	L	A	M	O		A	L	P	S
U	N	D	O		D	I	G	I	N		G	O	A	T
B	E	L	T		R	O	O	S	T		E	N	V	Y
S	W	E	E	P	I	N	G	C	H	A	N	G	E	
			I	F	S			E	D	T				
L	A	T	E	S	T		B	E	D	S		S	O	S
O	P	E	R	A		S	O	L	O		F	A	D	E
W	A	X	I	N	G	N	O	S	T	A	L	G	I	C
I	R	A	N		R	A	T	E		R	O	A	S	T
Q	T	S		P	I	G	S		C	R	E	S	T	S
		A	I	D			S	L	O					
D	U	S	T	I	N	G	P	O	W	D	E	R	S	
M	I	N	I		R	E	R	A	N		A	R	E	A
A	V	I	D		O	R	A	T	E		M	I	S	S
D	A	T	E		N	O	S	E	S		P	E	T	S

ABC

A	C		B
	B	A	C
B	A	C	
C		B	A

Clueless Crossword

E	X	C	I	T	E	S
V		R		R		I
A	M	U	S	I	N	G
S		M		V		H
I	M	P	R	I	N	T
O		L		A		E
N	E	E	D	L	E	D

Find the Ships

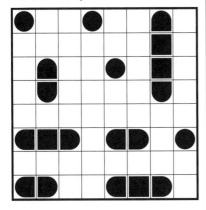

Betweener

How

Two-by-Four

Talc, navy

Cross That Bridge

P	O	P	S		D	O	T	S		C	R	A	M	S
A	R	E	A		A	L	O	T		H	A	N	O	I
W	I	S	H		L	E	E	R		I	N	G	O	T
N	O	T	A	B	I	G	D	E	A	L		E	S	S
S	N	O	R	E			S	P	E	L	L			
		A	T	F	I	R	S	T		A	H	M	E	
A	C	T		T	A	K	E		O	N	A	I	R	
D	O	E	S	O	N	E	S	B	I	D	D	I	N	G
D	I	N	E	R		T	O	L	D		R	I	O	
S	L	O	E		I	N	S	O	L	E	S			
		C	R	E	D	O				S	E	L	E	S
A	T	L		D	O	N	A	L	D	T	R	U	M	P
R	H	O	D	E		F	L	U	E		I	N	C	A
M	A	C	O	N		A	S	A	P		A	G	E	R
Y	I	K	E	S		T	O	U	T		L	E	E	K

Flight Formation

Small Change

Hot stuff

Fences

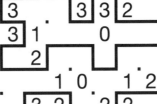

Initial Reaction

Let bygones be bygones.

Wrong Is Right

B) sargeant (should be *sergeant*)

Get the Door

S	T	A	M	P		S	P	A	T		T	E	A	S
A	O	L	E	R		L	U	L	U		H	O	S	E
G	R	A	N	O	L	A	B	A	R		U	N	I	T
S	E	N		M	U	M	S		K	A	N	S	A	S
			C	O	B	S		W	E	L	D			
S	E	D	A	T	E		J	A	Y	L	E	N	O	
E	L	O	P	E	D		E	L	S		R	A	F	T
A	B	U	T			E	L	K			B	I	T	E
T	O	G	A		O	W	L		G	R	O	V	E	S
	W	H	I	T	N	E	Y		R	E	L	E	N	T
		N	E	A	R		P	A	C	T				
C	A	S	H	E	W		A	U	T	O		G	A	S
O	R	E	O		H	A	M	M	E	R	L	O	C	K
S	I	L	O		I	H	O	P		D	E	L	H	I
T	A	L	K		M	A	S	S		S	A	F	E	S

Sudoku

3	9	4	2	1	5	6	8	7
5	8	1	4	6	7	9	3	2
6	2	7	9	3	8	5	4	1
7	5	6	1	4	9	8	2	3
9	4	2	7	8	3	1	6	5
8	1	3	5	2	6	7	9	4
1	6	5	3	9	2	4	7	8
2	7	9	8	5	4	3	1	6
4	3	8	6	7	1	2	5	9

Mixagrams

```
S I N E W    L A S H
R O N D O    V I S A
E R R O R    P U R R
S L E E K    W A R D
```

Page 34

123

3	1	2	3	1	2
1	2	3	1	2	3
2	3	1	2	3	1
3	1	2	3	1	2
1	2	3	1	2	3
2	3	1	2	3	1

Who's What Where?
A) Oxonian

Sound Thinking
Unbuckle

Page 35

For the Youngsters

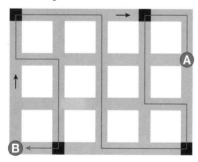

Page 36

One-Way Streets

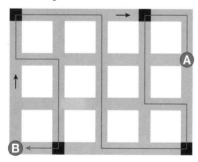

Addition Switch
186 + 649 = 835

Page 37

Missing Links

Say It Again
Cow

Page 38

Star Search

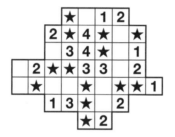

Choice Words
Harass, pester, bother

Page 39

Story Time

AHAS STAG WHERE
CAMP ARIA OARED
THEUGLYDUCKLING
SANDRA EDU FETE
IDS YRS
INKSPOTS BOPEEP
DEAN IRIS MERGE
THREELITTLEPIGS
ARMED PARA SCOT
GUARDS RUSSIANS
YEP MVP
WWII ALI EUREKA
HANSELANDGRETEL
AGILE NOVA STEM
METER ENDS TENS

Page 40

Line Drawing

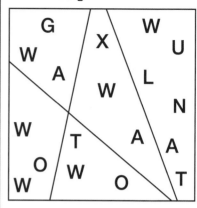

Wag, wow, wax, two, walnut

Three of a Kind
He s**cow**led at **the n**ot-at-all tasteful **jewe**lry (cow, hen, ewe).

In Other Words
Avuncular

Page 41

ABC

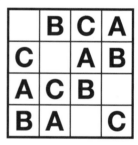

Two-by-Four
Gene, whiz

Page 42

Land Development

VOTED PLAN ATMS
AWARE AUTO SHOE
SECRETPLOT HALT
TSK PEAL STONES
MESS QUIRK
MASONS TREESAP
ARABS FLIER ARE
RELY RIP BLOT
SNL WAITS LOOSE
HAYRIDE MISTER
FINDS GELS
SHINER AHOY SEC
TIES ELBOWPATCH
IDLE SEES ALOHA
REDS SALT DEPOT

Page 43

Five by Five

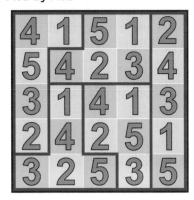

Small Change

Golf ball

Page 44

Find the Ships

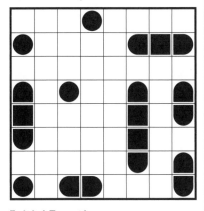

Initial Reaction

Don't rock the boat.

National Treasure

Again

Page 45

Sudoku

9	5	2	1	6	4	3	7	8
3	1	8	5	7	9	2	6	4
4	6	7	3	8	2	1	9	5
2	3	5	8	1	6	7	4	9
6	7	9	4	5	3	8	2	1
8	4	1	9	2	7	6	5	3
5	9	6	7	3	8	4	1	2
1	2	3	6	4	5	9	8	7
7	8	4	2	9	1	5	3	6

Mixagrams

```
S A M B A      F E U D
T A B O O      I M P S
A M O N G      D I A L
A D M A N      E G G S
```

Page 46

It's for You

Page 47

Fences

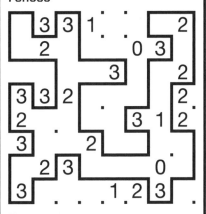

Betweener

Air

Wrong Is Right

C) vertabrate (should be *vertebrate*)

Page 48

Triad Split Decisions

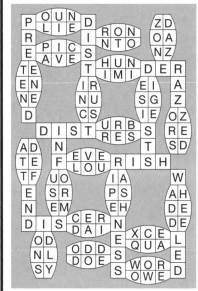

Transdeletion

Sleet

Page 49

123

1	3	2	3	1	2
3	2	1	2	3	1
1	3	2	1	2	3
2	1	3	2	3	1
3	2	1	3	1	2
2	1	3	1	2	3

Sudoku Sum

	13	14	18
19	8	2	9
17	4	7	6
9	1	5	3

Page 50

Animalistic

A	T	L	A	S		A	M	P	S		B	L	O	G
D	A	I	R	Y		P	O	L	E		L	U	R	E
D	R	E	A	M		A	R	E	A		A	L	A	N
S	T	U	B	B	O	R	N	A	S	A	M	U	L	E
			O	P	T			O	R	E				
P	E	B	B	L	E		L	E	N	O		S	O	B
E	A	R	L		R	I	O	S		M	A	N	N	A
P	R	O	U	D	A	S	A	P	E	A	C	O	C	K
S	E	W	E	R		A	N	N	A		T	R	U	E
I	D	S		Y	E	N	S		V	A	S	T	E	R
		S	U	M			M	E	L					
S	L	I	P	P	E	R	Y	A	S	A	N	E	E	L
T	I	D	E		R	E	A	L		R	A	N	T	O
A	M	E	N		G	I	R	L		M	I	C	R	O
B	E	A	T		E	N	D	S		S	L	E	E	T

Page 51

Number-Out

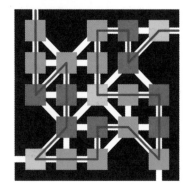

3	2	3	4	5
2	4	4	4	3
3	5	1	2	4
1	1	1	5	2
4	3	2	3	5

Think Alike
Save, keep

Who's What Where?
C) Thunder Bayite

Page 52

No Three in a Row

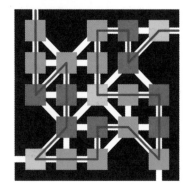

Say It Again
Fan

Page 53

Ellsworth

C	A	R	E	S		M	A	I	L		L	I	P	S
O	L	I	V	E		I	N	C	A		E	D	I	T
L	O	V	E	L	E	T	T	E	R		A	O	N	E
A	H	A		D	A	T	E		G	O	F	L	A	T
	A	L	L	O	T	S		S	E	L	L			
		E	M	U		S	T	R	E	E	T	S		
T	A	D	A		P	R	A	Y		O	T	H	E	R
S	L	E	D	S		O	W	L		S	T	E	E	D
P	L	A	I	T		W	E	E	P		U	M	P	S
		A	N	N	O	Y	E	D		E	T	C		
			G	R	I	D		H	A	V	E	A	T	
C	A	L	L	M	E		E	A	R	S		L	E	A
A	R	E	A		L	I	T	T	L	E	L	A	M	B
K	I	N	D		D	O	T	E		T	E	M	P	E
E	D	D	Y		S	U	E	D		S	T	O	O	D

Page 54

One-Way Streets

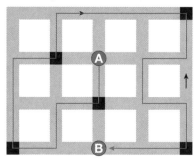

Sound Thinking
Payoff

Page 55

Hyper-Sudoku

1	9	6	5	4	2	3	7	8
3	5	4	8	9	7	6	2	1
8	2	7	3	6	1	9	5	4
7	6	1	9	5	3	4	8	2
9	4	8	2	7	6	5	1	3
2	3	5	4	1	8	7	6	9
4	1	9	6	8	5	2	3	7
6	8	2	7	3	9	1	4	5
5	7	3	1	2	4	8	9	6

Century Marks
25, 30, 26, 19

Page 56

Star Search

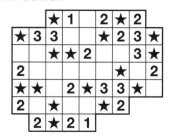

Choice Words
Arcane, secret, veiled

Page 57

Discoveries

P	E	R	U		S	P	I	C	Y		S	H	E	D
O	M	E	N		H	O	N	O	R		T	A	P	E
R	I	B	S		A	L	A	N	S		O	P	E	N
T	R	A	C	K	D	O	W	N		R	O	P	E	S
			R	E	E	S	E		P	A	G	E		
A	S	C	E	N	D			L	I	N	E	N	S	
S	T	O	W		S	T	I	N	G			U	K	E
H	A	M		M	A	T	I	N	E	E		P	U	N
E	R	E		A	G	A	P	E			P	O	N	D
	T	A	N	K	E	R			T	H	A	N	K	S
		C	O	E	D		R	A	R	E	R			
F	O	R	T	S		F	I	G	U	R	E	O	U	T
A	H	O	Y		P	I	P	E	S		N	A	S	A
R	I	S	E		E	V	E	N	T		T	H	E	M
M	O	S	T		T	E	N	T	S		S	U	D	S

Page 58

ABC

Clueless Crossword

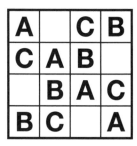

Page 59

Porcine Pair

Betweener

Bar

Page 60

Sudoku

2	1	7	5	3	6	8	9	4
9	8	3	1	4	2	6	7	5
5	4	6	7	8	9	2	1	3
4	5	1	9	6	3	7	8	2
7	6	2	4	1	8	3	5	9
3	9	8	2	7	5	1	4	6
1	7	9	3	2	4	5	6	8
8	3	5	6	9	1	4	2	7
6	2	4	8	5	7	9	3	1

Mixagrams

```
E D G E D     B O I L
G R O W N     H E R O
S A H I B     P O E T
S W O R D     A L A S
```

Page 61

Dental Work

Page 62

Line Drawing

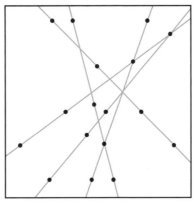

Three of a Kind

Don't **ask** me to **chore**ograph the Ban**jo B**and Ballet (task, chore, job).

Page 63

Find the Ships

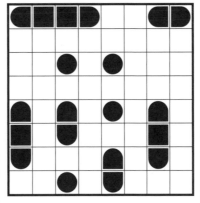

Two-by-Four

Mayo, unto

Page 64

Fences

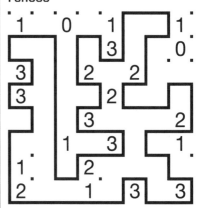

Addition Switch

$232 + 496 = 728$

Page 65

News Items

E	R	A	S		S	T	O	P	S		C	H	A	T
V	E	R	A		A	G	I	L	E		H	E	R	O
A	T	O	M		F	I	L	E	T		A	R	M	Y
D	O	U	B	L	E	F	E	A	T	U	R	E		
E	S	S	A	Y			R	T	E	S		D	O	G
S	S	E		R	O	D		S	E	A	S	I	D	E
		M	I	X	E	D			I	T	E	M		
	S	E	C	O	N	D	S	T	O	R	Y			
R	A	H	S		T	O	O	N	S					
E	R	A	S	U	R	E		D	O	T		P	A	S
P	E	N		S	E	C	T		A	L	E	R	T	
	G	O	O	D	L	U	C	K	P	I	E	C	E	
E	C	H	O		T	A	L	O	N		B	R	A	N
L	E	A	P		A	I	S	L	E		R	E	D	O
L	E	I	S		G	R	A	D	E		A	D	E	S

Page 66

123

3	2	1	2	3	1	2	3	1
1	3	2	3	1	2	3	1	2
3	2	3	1	2	3	1	2	1
2	1	2	3	1	2	3	1	3
1	3	1	2	3	1	2	3	2
2	1	2	3	1	2	3	1	3
3	2	3	1	2	3	1	2	1
1	3	1	2	3	1	2	3	2
2	1	3	1	2	3	1	2	3

Wrong Is Right

A) spattula (should be *spatula*)

Page 67

Number-Out

3	1	4	2	2
4	1	5	3	3
5	1	2	3	4
4	2	1	3	5
2	4	3	1	2

In Other Words
However

Think Alike
Hot, spicy

Page 68

Ante Up

```
 L A C E   T A T A   A R I D
S E W O N   H O E D   P O N E
C A L L E D O N E S B L U F F
I F S O   A M E N   A U T O S
      R E B A   S I N S
A L T E R   S K I D S   B U S
G O O D I E   N E T   P O P E
A S K I N G F O R A R A I S E
T E E N   G O T   G E Y S E R
E R N   H O R S E   D I E T S
      F A N G   L I O N
C H I L I   E R A S   G N A T
R E T U R N T O T H E F O L D
A R A T   P I L E   B O N E S
M O L E   R T E S   B R O S
```

Page 69

Sequence Maze

Say It Again
Nod

Page 70

Split Decisions

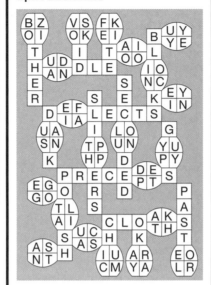

Transdeletion
Bottle

Page 71

Hyper-Sudoku

5	7	6	8	1	3	9	4	2
8	3	1	2	9	4	7	5	6
2	4	9	5	7	6	3	8	1
4	8	7	6	3	9	1	2	5
6	9	2	1	4	5	8	7	3
3	1	5	7	2	8	4	6	9
1	6	4	9	5	7	2	3	8
7	2	8	3	6	1	5	9	4
9	5	3	4	8	2	6	1	7

Mixagrams

```
C H A F E   L O O M
S A L A D   P U M A
P I E C E   L E S S
P A C E R   S O A K
```

Page 72

Sticky Stuff

```
A L P S   O P A L S   C H A T
N O A H   G E N I E   H O B O
T A P E P L A Y E R   A N E W
S M A L L E R   V A L E T S
      T A R   T R I C K Y
A S P E N S   R A N T   B U S
S M A R T   S I N G S   U N O
H A S   A P T   N I L
E S T   I G L O O   C A C T I
S H E   C O E D   B A T H E D
  B L O O M S   A L L
A R O U N D   I S L A N D S
F E A R   J A M S E S S I O N
R A R E   O B O E S   E L L A
O D D S   B E S E T   S E E P
```

Page 73

One-Way Streets

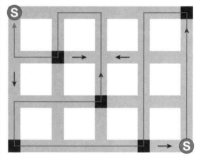

Sound Thinking
Origin

Page 74

Tanks a Lot

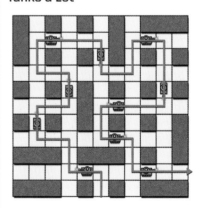

Small Change
Folk song

Gee-ography

P	A	P	A		M	D	C	L		M	A	R	S	H
A	P	E	R		E	R	I	E		A	L	O	H	A
G	E	R	M	A	N	Y	A	N	D	G	A	B	O	N
E	X	T	O	L		C	O	D	A		C	E	O	S
		R	I	L	E		L	I	S	A				
S	P	R	Y		I	R	A		S	P	R	A	N	G
A	A	A		A	R	E	N	A		U	T	T	E	R
G	U	Y	A	N	A	A	N	D	G	R	E	E	C	E
A	L	O	U	D		L	O	H	A	N		I	K	E
S	A	N	D	E	R		Y	E	T		I	N	S	T
		I	S	E	E		R	E	N	T				
H	A	T	E		A	X	L	E		A	C	T	O	R
G	R	E	N	A	D	A	A	N	D	G	H	A	N	A
T	E	A	C	H		L	I	C	E		E	X	E	C
V	A	S	E	S		T	R	E	E		D	I	S	K

Star Search

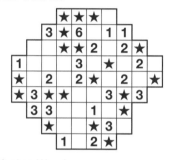

Choice Words

Bowler, fedora, helmet

Triad Split Decisions

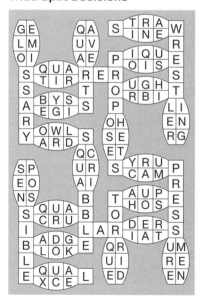

Transdeletion

Minute

Kitchen Set

U	T	A	H		H	O	M	E	S		B	I	D	S
N	O	R	A		E	V	E	R	T		E	D	I	E
F	R	O	N	T	R	A	N	G	E		A	L	A	W
I	S	M		H	O	L	D		P	A	N	E	L	S
T	O	A	D	I	E	S		B	O	S	C			
			I	N	S		V	A	N	P	O	O	L	S
A	M	A	S	S		T	I	K	I		U	R	A	L
M	E	S	H		M	O	N	E	T		N	E	R	O
I	O	T	A		A	W	E	D		S	T	O	K	E
S	W	I	N	D	L	E	S		M	A	E			
		T	E	A	R		R	E	F	R	A	C	T	
C	H	E	E	S	Y		S	A	M	E		S	H	E
H	O	R	N		S	I	N	K	O	R	S	W	I	M
E	B	O	N		I	C	I	E	R		R	A	M	P
R	O	S	A		A	U	T	R	Y		O	N	E	S

ABC

National Treasure

Banana

Find the Ships

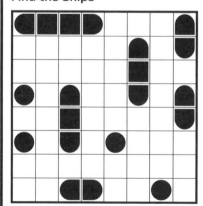

Two-by-Four

Bola, holy; ahoy, boll; ally, hobo

Plane Speaking

P	L	A	T	E		E	L	I	E		M	I	T	
S	A	L	O	N		N	E	L	L		L	A	M	A
S	M	O	O	T	H	T	A	L	K		E	R	A	S
T	E	E	N	I	E	R		S	A	V	A	G	E	
			T	R	Y	S	T		D	E	T	E	R	
R	A	F	F	L	E		T	O	T	A	L			
E	X	I	L	E		T	A	T	A		B	A	E	Z
E	L	S	A		W	A	T	E	R		E	L	L	A
L	E	T	T		O	P	U	S		A	S	I	A	N
	B	O	W	E	R		M	E	T	T	L	E		
Z	A	I	R	E		R	E	F	E	R				
I	G	N	O	R	E		I	N	A	R	A	G	E	
P	I	N	K		E	V	E	N	S	T	E	V	E	N
P	L	I	E		L	I	L	I		E	M	E	N	D
Y	E	S		Y	A	M	S		S	I	R	E	S	

Two Pairs

Betweener

Door

Sudoku

7	6	2	9	3	4	8	1	5
3	1	8	7	2	5	4	6	9
5	9	4	6	8	1	7	2	3
9	8	1	2	4	7	3	5	6
6	4	5	3	1	9	2	7	8
2	3	7	5	6	8	1	9	4
1	2	3	4	9	6	5	8	7
4	7	9	8	5	2	6	3	1
8	5	6	1	7	3	9	4	2

Mixagrams

V	I	E	W	S		T	H	U	S
B	A	S	I	S		I	R	O	N
A	L	O	N	E		P	R	I	G
R	O	U	G	E		S	P	A	T

Page 84

Fences

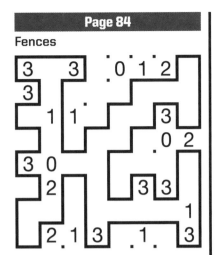

Wrong Is Right

C) auxilary (should be *auxiliary*)

Page 85

Fowl Language

S	W	A	G		M	E	S	S		M	A	K	E	R
H	E	R	O		A	R	I	A		A	T	A	R	I
O	R	E	O		T	U	R	K	E	Y	T	R	O	T
P	E	A	S	O	U	P		I	M	P	U	L	S	E
		E	A	R	T	H		B	O	N				
A	D	H	E	R	E		O	M	E	L	E	T	S	
B	R	I	G	S		G	L	A	D	E		H	A	H
B	A	N	G		C	E	L	T	S		D	A	R	E
A	I	D		C	O	T	E	S		L	U	N	G	E
	N	U	C	L	E	A	R		M	O	C	K	E	D
			H	U	R		S	T	O	R	K			
A	S	K	A	N	C	E		R	U	D	D	E	R	S
C	H	I	C	K	E	N	O	U	T		O	R	A	L
T	I	T	H	E		I	N	C	H		W	I	R	E
S	M	E	A	R		D	E	E	S		N	E	E	D

Page 86

Number-Out

Initial Reaction

A new broom sweeps clean.

Think Alike

Box, crate

Page 87

Hyper-Sudoku

5	3	4	1	8	2	6	9	7
6	8	2	7	4	9	5	3	1
7	9	1	3	5	6	2	4	8
3	6	5	4	9	8	1	7	2
9	2	7	6	1	5	3	8	4
4	1	8	2	3	7	9	5	6
1	4	6	9	7	3	8	2	5
8	7	3	5	2	1	4	6	9
2	5	9	8	6	4	7	1	3

Century Marks

8, 20, 60, 12

Page 88

On Your Feet

O	P	C	I	T		E	L	M	S		R	A	C	E
B	O	R	N	E		R	E	A	L		E	W	A	N
S	T	A	R	E		U	N	T	O		C	A	R	T
	G	E	T	U	P	T	H	E	N	E	R	V	E	
			E	S	T			O	D	D	E	R		
M	A	T	U	R	E		S	L	A	V	E			
A	L	E	S		S	U	A	V	E		A	R	F	
S	T	A	N	D	A	N	D	D	E	L	I	V	E	R
T	O	M		A	R	I	S	E		N	O	N	E	
			N	U	T	T	Y		P	A	N	N	E	D
		G	R	A	I	N		C	A	N				
	R	I	S	E	T	O	S	T	A	R	D	O	M	
E	P	I	C		R	A	I	N		H	A	I	L	S
C	O	D	E		A	G	E	D		O	T	T	E	R
O	N	E	S		N	A	R	Y		W	H	E	T	S

Page 89

Sets of Three

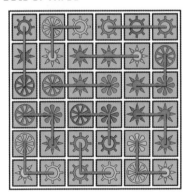

Say It Again

Plot

Page 90

One-Way Streets

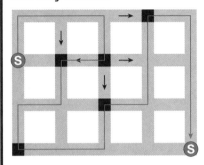

Sound Thinking

Soufflé

Page 91

Wrecking Crew

M	I	L	L	S		J	U	L	E	P		H	A	L
A	D	I	E	U		O	S	A	K	A		E	D	O
C	O	D	E	B	R	E	A	K	E	R		A	H	A
		W	O	L	F	E		T	A	R	O	T		
S	N	A	P	A	T			S	N	I	T	C	H	
P	A	R	T	Y	C	R	A	S	H	E	R			
I	D	E	A	S		E	N	T	E	R		D	E	B
T	E	N	S		B	I	T	E	S		M	E	M	O
E	R	A		D	U	G	I	N		F	E	N	C	E
			B	R	O	N	C	O	B	U	S	T	E	R
O	S	P	R	E	Y			E	R	A	S	E	S	
C	H	A	O	S		A	P	I	A	N				
T	I	N		S	A	F	E	C	R	A	C	K	E	R
E	N	D		E	L	A	T	E		C	H	I	N	A
T	E	A		D	A	R	E	S		E	A	T	E	N

Page 92

123

3	1	2	3	1	2	3	2	1
2	3	1	2	3	1	2	1	3
1	2	3	1	2	3	1	3	2
3	1	2	3	1	2	3	2	1
2	3	1	2	3	1	2	1	3
3	1	2	3	1	2	3	2	1
1	2	3	1	2	3	1	3	2
2	3	1	2	3	1	2	1	3
1	2	3	1	2	3	1	3	2

Three of a Kind

The **nick**el-plated gar**den t**ool is used for wee**ding** (nick, dent, ding).

Page 93

Line Drawing

Earn, hint, inch, kick, oath, omit

Sudoku Sum

	24	9	12
14	7	1	6
13	8	3	2
18	9	5	4

Page 94

Triple Treat

S	H	I	E	D		O	P	E	D		I	M	A	M
T	I	T	L	E		T	A	R	A		D	I	N	E
D	R	E	S	S	S	H	I	R	T		E	S	T	D
S	E	M	E	S	T	E	R		E	R	A	S	E	S
			E	A	R		B	L	A	S	S			
B	O	G	A	R	T		S	L	I	T		A	P	B
S	P	R	I	T		S	T	O	N	E		I	R	A
I	T	A	L		S	P	I	N	E		I	G	O	R
D	I	S		L	U	R	E	D		M	O	O	S	E
E	N	S		A	G	E	S		S	I	N	N	E	R
			S	I	N	G	E		A	I	M			
O	U	T	A	G	E		A	P	P	O	I	N	T	S
S	H	A	M		S	W	I	S	S	S	T	E	A	K
L	U	I	S		T	I	N	E		A	C	U	T	E
O	H	N	O		S	E	T	S		S	H	R	E	D

Page 95

Star Search

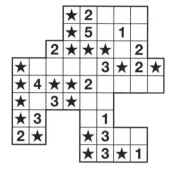

Choice Words

Apache, Navajo, Paiute

Page 96

Dicey

Small Change

Hush money

Page 97

Fasten-ation

R	O	I	L	S		M	A	P	S		R	G	T
E	B	O	O	K		A	L	S	O		V	E	R	O
B	O	W	L	I	N	G	P	I	N		I	C	A	N
S	E	A		B	O	O	S		A	D	D	U	C	E
			O	O	O		S	T	E	E	R	E	D
P	R	O	T	O	N		C	H	I	N	O			
L	I	G	H	T		S	O	O	N		T	O	R	I
E	C	R	U		P	I	N	T	A		A	V	O	N
D	E	E	M		A	L	A	S		S	P	E	A	R
			B	A	R	O	N		S	T	E	R	N	E
M	O	A	N	E	R	S		R	A	E			
A	R	C	A	R	O		G	A	S	P		A	S	H
T	A	T	I		T	O	O	T	H	P	A	S	T	E
E	L	A	L		E	R	I	E		E	V	I	A	N
S	S	S		D	O	N	S		S	E	A	R	S

Page 98

Hyper-Sudoku

9	4	2	8	3	5	1	6	7
1	8	3	7	4	6	5	2	9
7	6	5	9	2	1	3	4	8
6	2	1	4	5	9	8	7	3
5	3	7	1	8	2	4	9	6
4	9	8	3	6	7	2	1	5
3	1	6	5	7	4	9	8	2
8	7	4	2	9	3	6	5	1
2	5	9	6	1	8	7	3	4

Mixagrams

C R E D O	H E R B
O D D L Y	A I D E
R E V U E	B O W L
N U R S E	D E B T

Page 99

ABC

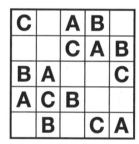

C		A	B
	C	A	B
B	A		C
A	C	B	
	B		C	A

National Treasure

Guyana

Page 100

All Talk

A	S	S	E	T		S	E	E	M		P	L	U	M
H	I	P	P	O		A	X	L	E		R	I	P	E
A	R	E	A	S		T	I	L	L		E	V	E	N
B	E	A		S	T	A	T	E	O	F	M	I	N	D
	K	L	E	I	N		D	R	E	A	D	S		
G	R	E	A	S	E		F	R	I	E	D			
L	O	A	N		S	P	R	U	C	E		V	I	P
A	S	S	E	S		A	O	L		S	T	O	N	E
D	A	Y		C	A	N	N	E	S		R	I	C	E
			S	O	W	E	D		I	C	E	C	A	P
D	E	S	I	R	E		A	G	R	E	E			
E	X	P	R	E	S	S	L	I	N	E		O	N	O
M	I	L	E		O	P	E	D		D	I	V	E	R
O	L	I	N		M	A	D	E		I	D	E	A	L
N	E	T	S		E	R	A	S		T	A	R	R	Y

Page 101

Find the Ships

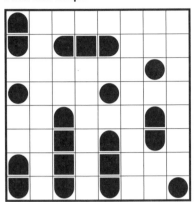

Betweener

Folk

Two-by-Four

Club, sumo

Page 102

Triad Split Decisions

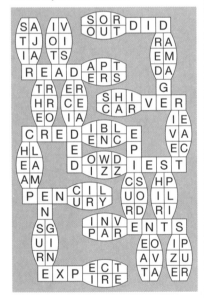

Transdeletion

Air bag

Page 103

Two for You

S	I	E	G	E		D	E	E	M		S	A	P	S
G	O	R	E	S		I	D	E	A		A	V	O	N
T	W	I	N	E	N	G	I	N	E	P	L	A	N	E
S	A	N	E		O	U	T		L	A	N	C	E	
		P	R	O	P		C	H	A	R	T	E	R	
B	A	B	O	O	N		C	R	O	N	Y			
E	L	I	O	T		S	L	A	W		C	D	S	
D	U	A	L	C	I	T	I	Z	E	N	S	H	I	P
E	M	S		M	I	N	E		O	N	I	C	E	
	D	R	A	N	G		C	L	O	N	E	D		
L	A	R	A	I	N	E		S	L	O	W			
A	F	O	U	L		D	E	E		S	W	A	M	
D	O	U	B	L	E	O	R	N	O	T	H	I	N	G
E	R	T	E		B	R	A	S		N	O	S	I	R
S	E	E	D		B	E	B	E		T	E	E	N	S

Page 104

123

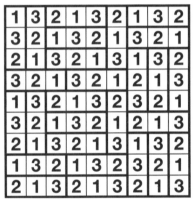

1	3	2	1	3	2	1	3	2
3	2	1	3	2	1	3	2	1
2	1	3	2	1	3	1	3	2
3	2	1	3	2	1	2	1	3
1	3	2	1	3	2	3	2	1
3	2	1	3	2	1	2	1	3
2	1	3	2	1	3	1	3	2
1	3	2	1	3	2	3	2	1
2	1	3	2	1	3	2	1	3

Wrong Is Right

B) aquiescent (should be *acquiescent*)

Page 105

Fences

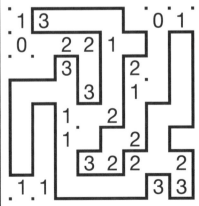

Addition Switch

776 + 108 = 884

Page 106

Compromise

L	A	V	E	R		S	P	E	C		S	T	A	B
A	L	I	V	E		P	L	E	A		H	A	L	E
G	I	V	E	G	R	O	U	N	D		O	K	I	E
S	T	A	R		E	D	S		I	N	V	E	N	T
		M	A	L	E		F	L	E	E	C	E	S	
A	N	T	O	N	Y		R	E	L	I	S	H		
B	O	A	R	D		T	O	T	A	L		A	R	M
L	U	K	E		F	O	L	I	C		P	R	A	Y
E	N	E		C	A	K	E	D		L	O	G	I	N
	F	L	U	K	E	S		S	E	L	E	N	A	
G	E	L	A	T	I	N		S	O	I	L			
A	R	I	S	E	N		E	C	O		S	L	A	P
Z	I	G	S		G	I	V	E	N	O	T	I	C	E
E	C	H	O		I	V	A	N		P	E	R	I	L
R	A	T	S		T	E	S	T		T	R	A	D	E

Page 107

A Froggy Day

Say It Again

Ring

Page 108

Hyper-Sudoku

1	6	7	4	2	9	3	5	8
5	2	4	7	3	8	1	9	6
8	9	3	5	1	6	2	4	7
4	8	1	6	9	5	7	3	2
3	5	9	1	7	2	6	8	4
2	7	6	3	8	4	5	1	9
6	1	5	9	4	7	8	2	3
7	4	8	2	5	3	9	6	1
9	3	2	8	6	1	4	7	5

Mixagrams

I	N	F	E	R		C	U	B	E
F	L	U	T	E		S	T	A	R
M	E	L	E	E		T	A	C	K
S	P	L	I	T		O	A	K	S

Page 109

Car Wear

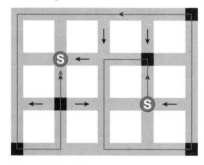

R	O	S	I	E		C	A	W	S		T	I	N	A
A	L	A	R	M		A	L	O	E		I	R	O	N
G	E	T	M	E		T	A	L	C		M	A	S	T
	G	E	A	R	S	H	I	F	T		I	T	I	S
		G	U	Y			O	R	N	E	R	Y		
G	O	P	H	E	R		S	P	R	I	G			
E	P	E	E		F	A	T	E		B	B	A	L	L
L	I	L	A	C		B	E	N		S	E	P	I	A
S	E	T	T	O		L	I	N	K		L	O	R	D
			E	L	L	E	N		N	E	T	P	A	Y
C	H	O	R	A	L			S	E	A				
L	A	T	H		B	R	A	K	E	S	H	O	E	
A	S	T	O		E	A	V	E		T	A	L	L	Y
U	T	E	S		A	V	I	D		E	R	A	S	E
S	O	R	E		N	E	S	S		R	E	F	E	R

Page 110

One-Way Streets

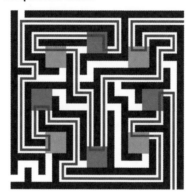

Sound Thinking

Charade

Page 111

Star Search

	★	3	★		1		1	
		★			★		★	
★	4	★	3	2			★	3	★
	3	5	★		★		2		2
★	★	3	★	3	2		★	2	★
★	3	2			★	2	★	3	3
1					2			★	
				★		1		
				★	2		

Choice Words

Banana, cherry, orange

Page 112

Contain Yourself

M	E	A	L		F	A	L	S	E		B	M	O	C
A	X	L	E		O	N	I	O	N		E	U	R	O
J	U	G	G	E	R	N	A	U	T		A	G	E	R
O	D	E		M	E	I	R		W	A	R	G	O	D
R	E	R	A	I	S	E		H	I	N	D	I		
			G	L	A	S	S	I	N	E		N	F	C
T	V	C	R	E	W		C	H	E	W		E	L	I
A	A	A	A		S	R	O			P	S	A	T	
X	I	N		E	S	A	U		C	I	A	S	P	Y
I	N	N		C	U	P	B	O	A	R	D			
		O	D	O	R	S		D	R	E	S	S	E	R
C	A	N	I	N	E		P	E	O	N		U	M	A
H	O	A	X		B	O	T	T	L	E	N	E	C	K
U	N	D	O		E	L	A	T	E		I	D	E	E
B	E	E	N		T	A	S	E	R		L	E	E	S

Page 113

Sequence Maze

Small Change

Layer cake

Page 114

Sudoku

1	8	7	9	5	6	2	4	3
3	2	9	8	1	4	5	6	7
4	6	5	3	7	2	8	1	9
6	9	8	2	3	1	7	5	4
7	3	2	5	4	9	6	8	1
5	4	1	7	6	8	9	3	2
8	1	3	6	2	7	4	9	5
9	7	4	1	8	5	3	2	6
2	5	6	4	9	3	1	7	8

Century Marks

19, 29, 39, 13

Page 115

Think Fast

S	H	A	D		C	H	A	N		A	C	R	I	D
H	U	M	E		L	O	B	E		C	L	A	R	E
A	M	B	I		A	P	E	R		E	X	P	O	S
Q	U	I	C	K	S	I	L	V	E	R		I	N	K
	S	T	E	P	S			E	M	B	E	D		
			H	I	P	S			T	I	N	C	A	N
S	P	F	S		C	I	T	E		C	R	I	M	E
T	A	L	L		S	A	R	A	H		O	T	I	S
A	T	E	I	N		F	A	R	O		L	Y	E	S
R	E	E	D	I	T		P	L	O	Y				
			T	E	C	H	S			P	E	S	T	O
M	A	R		E	X	P	R	E	S	S	I	O	N	S
E	N	A	C	T		L	I	L	T		T	R	I	O
R	O	T	O	R		I	D	L	E		A	S	O	F
E	N	E	M	Y		T	E	A	R		R	O	N	A

Page 116

Split Decisions

Transdeletion

Austin

Page 117

Number-Out

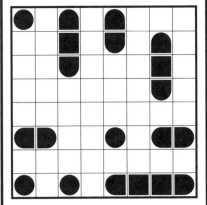

Who's What Where?
C) Allentonian

Think Alike
Adore, love

Page 118

Prize Cries

P	A	R	T		S	P	A	S		S	C	O	F	F
O	V	E	R		L	A	N	A		N	O	M	A	D
N	A	V	E		A	T	T	N		A	N	I	T	A
C	L	E	A	R	T	H	E	D	E	C	K	S		
H	O	R	D	E			A	R	K		S	O	B	
O	N	T		L	I	T	T	L	E		F	I	N	E
		T	I	A	R	A		B	O	O	Z	E		
	W	E	R	E	N	U	M	B	E	R	O	N	E	
B	O	N	U	S			P	I	L	O	T			
R	O	S	E		D	R	A	G	I	N		P	B	S
O	D	E		E	R	A			T	O	L	E	T	
	M	O	V	E	T	O	T	H	E	R	E	A	R	
C	O	B	R	A		E	L	I	A		G	A	T	E
A	L	L	A	N		D	E	N	S		A	S	I	S
P	E	E	L	S		R	O	T	H		N	E	T	S

Page 119

ABC

Three of a Kind
So, let's se**arch** for **the el**usive buried treasure (sole, arch, heel).

Page 120

Find the Ships

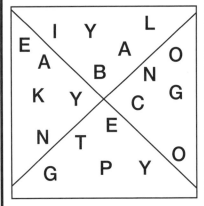

Two-by-Four
Drug, dyer

Page 121

Line Drawing

Congo, Egypt, Kenya, Libya

Clueless Crossword

G	I	Z	Z	A	R	D
A		E		R		E
R	E	P	O	R	T	S
B		H		I		E
L	A	Y	O	V	E	R
E		R		E		T
D	E	S	I	S	T	S

Page 122

High Spirits

W	A	N	D		A	D	O	B	E		R	I	L	E
O	L	E	O		L	A	M	A	S		U	N	I	V
K	E	R	N		P	L	A	N	S		M	A	K	E
S	C	O	T	C	H	I	N	G		A	B	N	E	R
		L	O	A			O	P	U	L	E	N	T	
T	R	A	I	N		C	U	R	A	T	E			
W	I	N	E	S	A	P	S		Y	O	D	U	D	E
I	P	O		M	A	U	D	E			S	U	N	
G	A	N	G	U	P		R	Y	E	B	R	E	A	D
		I	N	L	A	Y	S		L	O	R	D	S	
P	O	I	N	T	E	R		C	A	B				
L	I	N	G	O		B	O	U	R	B	O	N	S	T
A	L	L	A		N	O	T	R	E		T	O	U	R
T	E	E	M		B	R	I	G	S		I	N	D	O
E	R	T	E		A	S	S	E	T		C	O	S	T

Page 123

Looped Path

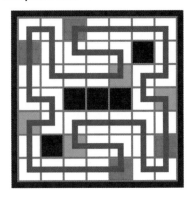

Betweener
Meal

Page 124

Hyper-Sudoku

6	1	9	2	4	7	5	8	3
4	3	8	6	5	1	7	2	9
7	2	5	9	3	8	6	4	1
8	4	7	1	2	9	3	5	6
1	6	3	5	7	4	2	9	8
9	5	2	3	8	6	4	1	7
3	8	6	4	1	5	9	7	2
5	9	1	7	6	2	8	3	4
2	7	4	8	9	3	1	6	5

Mixagrams

C A C H E   T R A Y
A S S A Y   K I C K
S O L V E   U P O N
E G R E T   G O W N

Page 125

Gridiron Action

S	A	N	D	S		T	R	A	M		G	A	L	E
C	L	A	I	M		A	E	R	O		A	V	I	A
U	L	T	R	A		B	E	A	N		L	E	E	R
B	A	T	T	L	E	O	F	B	U	L	L	R	U	N
A	N	Y		L	A	O	S		M	O	O			
			L	E	T	S		T	E	N	P	I	N	S
S	K	I	E	S		E	O	N			R	O	Y	
A	N	D	I	T	C	A	M	E	T	O	P	A	S	S
M	A	E		R	O	T		U	P	S	E	T		
S	P	A	T	I	A	L		S	A	T	S			
		R	O	C		H	E	A	R		W	O	O	
A	D	R	I	N	K	W	I	T	H	A	K	I	C	K
L	O	O	P		P	A	N	T		G	E	N	O	A
A	L	S	O		O	N	T	O		E	N	E	M	Y
S	L	E	D		T	E	S	S		D	O	S	E	S

Page 126

Fences

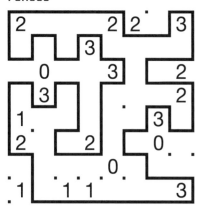

Wrong Is Right
D) clavacle (should be *clavicle*)

Page 127

Dotty

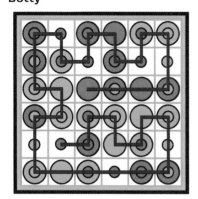

Say It Again
Seal

Page 128

Number-Out

3	6	2	1	5	5
2	4	4	4	3	6
4	2	5	6	1	1
3	3	3	5	2	1
1	4	6	4	2	2
5	1	2	3	6	6

In Other Words
Elixir

Think Alike
Brave, bold

Page 129

Principal Sounds

S	U	P	T		P	O	S	T		A	B	B	E	Y
O	S	L	O		A	N	T	I		R	O	U	S	E
L	E	A	F		S	E	E	N		E	G	Y	P	T
A	U	G	U	S	T	A	M	A	I	N	E			
R	P	I		T	E	L		N	A	Y	S	A	Y	
	A	V	I	D		P	O	T	S		P	T	A	
A	P	R	O	N		S	E	A	R		C	R	E	W
C	H	I	C	K	E	N	C	H	O	W	M	E	I	N
H	A	Z	E		L	U	A	U		R	O	A	N	S
E	S	E		S	I	G	N		M	I	N	D		
S	E	R	A	P	H		W	O	N		E	V	A	
		B	O	U	N	D	I	N	G	M	A	I	N	
L	A	B	O	R		A	U	L	D		E	G	A	D
A	L	E	R	T		B	E	L	A		E	L	L	E
D	E	N	T	S		S	L	A	Y		T	E	S	S

Page 130

123

1	3	2	3	1	2	3	2	1
2	1	3	1	2	3	1	3	2
3	2	1	2	3	1	2	1	3
1	3	2	1	2	3	1	3	2
3	1	3	2	1	2	3	2	1
1	2	1	3	2	3	2	1	3
2	3	2	1	3	1	3	2	1
3	2	1	3	1	2	1	3	2
2	1	3	2	3	1	2	1	3

Two-by-Four
Cyan, quip

Page 131

Find the Ships

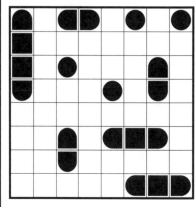

Sudoku Sum

	12	23	10
17	3	9	5
14	7	6	1
14	2	8	4

Page 132

Color Commentary

B	A	N	G		G	L	O	S	S		S	W	A	B
A	F	A	R		M	A	N	T	A		O	H	M	Y
B	L	U	E	S	T	R	E	A	K		L	I	F	E
K	A	R	E	N		I	N	G	E		A	T	M	S
A	T	U	N	E		A	D	E		A	R	E		
			B	E	S	T		M	S	G		S	U	P
R	O	B	E	R	T		C	O	N	T	R	A	S	T
O	K	L	A		A	R	O	M	A		E	L	S	A
B	R	A	N	D	N	E	W		F	A	D	E	R	S
S	A	C		A	D	S		C	U	R	S			
	K	E	Y		T	I	A		E	T	A	I	L	
L	A	B	S		E	A	R	N		N	A	N	N	Y
I	C	E	S		G	R	A	Y	M	A	T	T	E	R
E	L	L	A		G	E	N	O	A		E	I	R	E
D	U	T	Y		S	A	I	N	T		S	S	T	S

215

Page 133

Alternating Tiles

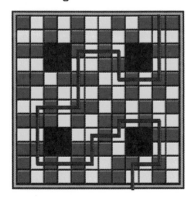

Small Change
Fair shake

Page 134

Star Search

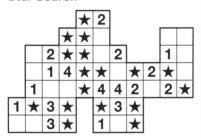

Choice Words
Accrue, garner, obtain

Page 135

Trunk Lines

C	H	A	D	■	C	E	L	T	S	■	O	M	A	R
N	O	M	E	■	O	M	A	H	A	■	W	A	D	E
B	L	I	P	■	A	M	M	A	N	■	E	P	I	C
C	E	D	A	R	R	A	P	I	D	S	■	L	E	A
■	■	L	A	S	■	■	S	C	A	R	E	U	P	■
R	O	O	M	I	E	S	T	■	R	Y	E	S	■	■
H	U	L	A	S	■	L	U	N	A	■	D	Y	E	D
E	T	D	■	A	L	I	B	A	B	A	■	R	U	E
A	S	H	E	■	E	T	A	T	■	E	X	U	R	B
■	■	I	N	T	O	■	S	O	F	T	S	P	O	T
P	U	C	C	I	N	I	■	■	R	N	A	■	■	■
A	C	K	■	A	U	S	T	R	I	A	N	O	A	K
T	O	O	T	■	R	U	S	E	S	■	D	A	T	E
I	N	R	E	■	I	Z	A	A	K	■	O	H	M	Y
O	N	Y	X	■	S	U	R	L	Y	■	S	U	E	S

Page 136

Sudoku

2	7	3	9	6	5	8	4	1
5	9	8	4	2	1	6	3	7
4	1	6	7	8	3	2	5	9
1	3	9	8	5	4	7	2	6
6	4	7	2	3	9	5	1	8
8	2	5	6	1	7	3	9	4
9	6	4	5	7	2	1	8	3
3	8	2	1	4	6	9	7	5
7	5	1	3	9	8	4	6	2

Mixagrams

```
U S H E R       S C A R
A G O N Y       S I R E
F I L M Y       A T O M
I D Y L L       B Y E S
```

Page 137

One-Way Streets

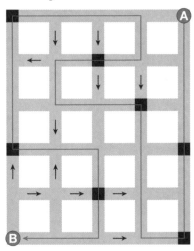

Sound Thinking
Seamstress

Page 138

ABC

		A	C	B
A	B	C		
C		B	A	
B	A			C
	C		B	A

Betweener
Other

National Treasure
Nomadic

Page 139

The Usual

B	A	Y	S	■	F	I	C	U	S	■	A	P	E
A	B	O	M	B	■	A	M	I	S	H	■	V	E	X
R	E	G	U	L	A	R	A	R	M	Y	■	E	R	A
■	T	I	D	E	S	■	X	C	I	■	C	R	O	C
■	■	G	A	S	P	■	E	N	C	H	A	N	T	■
E	T	C	E	T	E	R	A	■	T	H	U	G	■	■
L	E	O	■	S	N	I	P	S	■	A	M	E	B	A
B	A	M	■	T	O	P	U	P	■	J	O	N	■
A	R	M	E	D	■	R	A	D	A	R	■	O	A	T
■	■	O	R	E	S	■	L	A	Y	O	V	E	R	S
C	A	N	I	N	E	S	■	N	O	P	E	■	■
H	U	G	E	■	T	W	O	■	L	E	N	D	S	■
I	D	O	■	S	T	A	N	D	A	R	D	O	I	L
R	I	O	■	A	L	T	E	R	■	S	E	R	G	E
P	O	D	■	M	E	S	S	Y	■	D	A	N	G

Page 140

Find the Ships

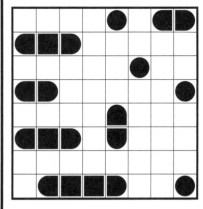

Two-by-Four
Gulf, hour

123

2	1	3	2	3	1	2	1	3
1	3	2	3	1	2	3	2	1
3	2	1	2	3	1	2	1	3
1	3	2	1	2	3	1	3	2
3	2	1	3	1	2	3	2	1
2	1	3	1	2	3	1	3	2
1	3	2	3	1	2	3	2	1
2	1	3	1	2	3	1	3	2
3	2	1	2	3	1	2	1	3

Addition Switch

320 + 377 = 697

Clean Slate

A	C	T	O	R		B	L	O	C		K	E	P	T
M	O	O	R	E		L	O	L	A		E	X	A	M
P	U	R	E	B	L	O	O	D	S		Y	A	L	E
S	P	E	C		O	W	N		H	A	N	S	E	N
		A	O	L			A	E	S	O	P			
S	P	A	R	K	L	I	N	G	W	A	T	E	R	
P	I	N		D	E	C	O	R		P	E	R	O	N
A	N	D	S		R	I	T	E	S		R	A	G	A
S	K	Y	E	S		C	R	E	A	M		T	U	T
	S	T	A	I	N	L	E	S	S	S	T	E	E	L
	A	L	G	A	E		H	U	H					
F	R	Y	I	N	G		B	O	A		R	E	B	A
L	I	L	O		S	N	O	W	Y	R	I	V	E	R
U	P	O	N		A	O	N	E		E	V	I	T	A
B	A	R	S		T	R	O	D		C	E	L	E	B

Fences

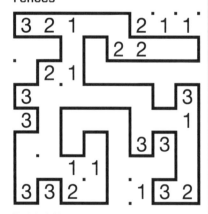

Initial Reaction

Half a loaf is better than none.

Wrong Is Right

A) eucalyptis (should be *eucalyptus*)

Number-Out

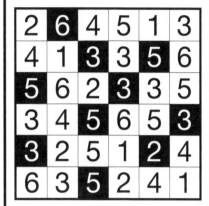

Think Alike

Soft, mushy

50 of a Kind

A	B	I	T		B	A	B	O	O		B	I	B	B
R	A	B	I		A	B	O	R	T		A	B	O	O
B	R	A	M		B	L	A	B	B	E	R	I	N	G
	B	R	E	A	K	E	R		B	O	D	E	S	
		B	S	A			E	B	A	N				
A	B	B	O	T		B	U	R	Y		R	E	B	
B	U	R	M	A		B	A	B	A		A	B	E	
F	L	I	B	B	E	R	T	I	G	I	B	B	E	T
A	L	B		B	I	T	E		S	A	B	R	A	
B	Y	E		B	O	D	Y		B	R	I	T	S	
		B	A	N	E		B	U	N					
C	B	E	R	S		B	A	R	T	A	B	S		
R	U	B	I	K	S	C	U	B	E		B	I	L	L
I	C	B	M		O	B	O	E	S		A	B	A	B
B	O	S	S		B	O	N	E	T		S	I	B	S

Straight Ahead

Betweener

Piece

Hyper-Sudoku

6	2	7	8	1	5	9	3	4
3	8	4	7	6	9	2	5	1
9	1	5	2	4	3	8	6	7
2	9	3	6	8	1	4	7	5
7	4	1	5	9	2	6	8	3
5	6	8	4	3	7	1	2	9
4	5	2	1	7	6	3	9	8
1	7	9	3	2	8	5	4	6
8	3	6	9	5	4	7	1	2

Mixagrams

S	O	N	I	C		M	O	T	H
S	C	A	N	T		I	R	I	S
E	V	E	N	T		M	A	M	A
C	A	R	O	L		A	H	E	M

Labor Paradox?

P	A	S	S		E	P	S	O	M		I	M	O	
A	W	A	Y		N	E	A	R	S		S	C	A	N
W	H	Y	D	I	D	T	H	E	U	S	M	I	N	T
N	I	H		G	R	I	L	L		E	I	E	I	O
S	T	E	P	O	U	T			E	X	T	R	A	
		Y	A	R	N		C	N	O	T	E			
Y	A	K	S		R	H	I	N	E		D	S	L	
U	N	I	O	N	G	O	O	N	S	T	R	I	K	E
M	A	D		O	U	T	I	E		H	A	I	G	
		F	L	Y	E	R		K	T	E	L			
	G	U	R	U	S		B	A	R	E	T	T	A	
S	O	N	I	C		G	H	A	N	A		O	R	B
T	O	M	A	K	E	L	E	S	S	M	O	N	E	Y
U	S	E	R		M	A	R	I	A		R	E	V	S
B	E	T		U	M	A	S	S		A	S	I	S	

Page 149

Triad Split Decisions

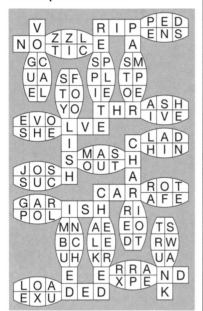

Transdeletion
"Blondie"

Page 150

One-Way Streets

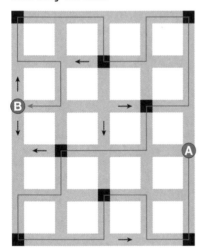

Sound Thinking
Outbound

Page 151

Fall Prelude

A	L	P		D	A	R	E	S		C	R	E	P	T
R	I	O		I	T	A	L	O		L	O	V	E	R
E	E	R		S	O	N	A	R		O	B	E	S	E
A	U	T	U	M	N	A	L	E	Q	U	I	N	O	X
		E	N	A	C	T			U	S	N			
C	A	N	D	L	E		B	R	I	E		S	P	A
A	R	T	I		M	E	H	T	A		E	E	C	
G	O	O	D	B	Y	E	T	O	S	U	M	M	E	R
E	M	U		R	E	N	T	S		I	N	D	Y	
D	A	S		I	N	D	Y		C	R	E	P	E	S
	A	N	T			C	L	O	T	H				
C	H	A	N	G	E	O	F	S	E	A	S	O	N	S
P	E	S	T	O		P	A	P	E	R		R	A	W
A	E	I	O	U		E	R	A	S	E		E	P	A
S	L	A	N	T		C	O	N	E	D		S	A	Y

Page 152

Solitaire Poker

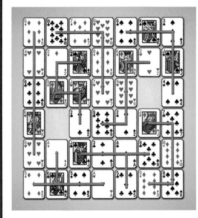

Say It Again
Coach, train

Page 153

Star Search

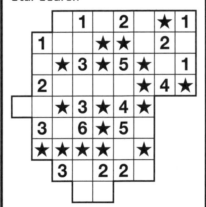

Choice Words
Calais, Nantes, Verdun

Page 154

Sudoku

5	4	7	1	6	3	8	2	9
1	8	3	2	9	5	4	7	6
6	9	2	7	4	8	1	3	5
9	3	4	6	7	1	5	8	2
7	5	1	3	8	2	9	6	4
8	2	6	4	5	9	3	1	7
2	6	8	5	1	4	7	9	3
4	7	9	8	3	6	2	5	1
3	1	5	9	2	7	6	4	8

Century Marks
36, 23, 13, 28

Page 155

Final Averages

A	C	L	U		H	A	L	T		P	A	N	G
L	H	A	S	A		O	L	E	O		I	G	O	R
T	A	K	E	T	O	M	E	A	N		G	A	T	E
O	P	E	R	A	T	E		D	E	S	P	I	S	E
			L	I	S	P			T	E	N	O	N	
S	P	O	I	L	S		R	E	C	O	N			
A	E	R	O		S	O	N	A	R		W	H	O	
S	T	A	N	D	U	P	C	O	M	E	D	I	A	N
H	E	N		A	R	I	E	S		O	S	L	O	
		S	U	I	T	E		F	A	T	H	E	R	
R	A	V	E	N		D	U	E	T					
A	B	E	T	T	O	R		R	E	L	A	T	E	D
C	A	R	T		P	I	E	A	L	A	M	O	D	E
E	S	S	E		E	L	A	L		S	I	N	G	E
S	E	E	R		N	E	T	S		D	Y	E	D	

Page 156

ABC

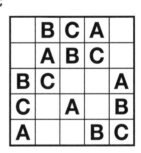

Two-by-Four
Beer, gave; berg, eave

218

Page 157

Find the Ships

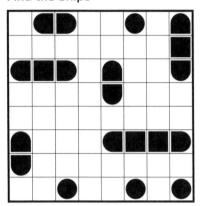

Clueless Crossword

T	R	E	A	D	L	E
H		N		E		S
I	N	F	A	N	T	S
E		O		T		E
V	E	R	S	I	O	N
E		C		S		C
S	H	E	A	T	H	E

Page 158

Onion Specific

Page 159

Dot to Dot

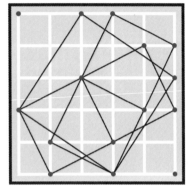

Small Change

Pipe dream

Page 160

123

3	1	2	1	2	3	1	2	3
1	2	3	2	3	1	2	3	1
2	3	1	3	1	2	3	1	2
1	2	3	1	2	3	1	2	3
2	3	1	2	3	1	2	3	1
3	1	2	3	1	2	3	1	2
1	2	3	2	3	1	2	3	1
2	3	1	3	1	2	3	1	2
3	1	2	1	2	3	1	2	3

Wrong Is Right

B) daquiri (should be *daiquiri*)

Page 161

Fences

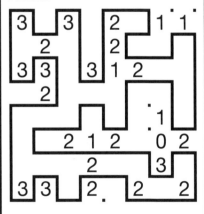

Sudoku Sum

	13	15	17
12	1	5	6
15	9	2	4
18	3	8	7

Page 162

Columbus Natives

Page 163

Hyper-Sudoku

8	5	4	7	6	3	9	1	2
1	3	2	8	5	9	4	7	6
9	6	7	1	4	2	5	3	8
2	4	9	5	7	1	6	8	3
3	1	8	2	9	6	7	5	4
5	7	6	3	8	4	1	2	9
4	8	1	9	2	5	3	6	7
6	2	5	4	3	7	8	9	1
7	9	3	6	1	8	2	4	5

Mixagrams

L	E	G	A	L	D	U	T	Y	
E	R	A	S	E	G	L	U	E	
A	P	A	R	T	P	L	E	A	
P	I	E	T	Y	U	S	E	R	

Page 164

Split Decisions

Transdeletion

Linguine

Page 165

Doin' Duos

G	A	R	B		P	R	A	M		D	A	C	C	A
L	U	A	U		H	I	F	I		U	S	H	E	R
O	D	I	N		O	G	R	E		R	H	I	N	E
M	I	L	K	I	N	H	O	N	E	Y		P	T	A
			B	R	E	T			L	E	A	P		
O	T	H	E	R	S		B	A	V	A	R	I	A	
P	R	I	D	E		S	E	M	I		C	N	B	C
T	U	T		G	E	T	L	O	S	T		D	O	A
S	E	T	S		D	A	I	S		A	C	I	D	S
	R	I	P	O	S	T	E		S	L	O	P	E	S
	N	Y	S	E			U	P	O	N				
T	O	M		C	L	E	A	N	I	N	J	E	R	K
A	K	I	T	A		A	V	I	D		O	L	A	N
R	I	S	E	R		V	O	T	E		I	S	T	O
P	E	S	T	S		E	W	E	R		N	E	S	T

Page 166

Tiki Mask

Betweener

Space

Page 167

Number-Out

6	6	5	4	2	1
5	4	2	6	1	3
3	4	6	4	5	4
2	5	6	2	6	4
2	1	4	1	3	4
6	3	3	5	1	2

Think Alike

Calm, serene

Page 168

One-Way Streets

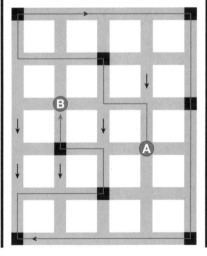

Page 169

Leading Phrase

P	O	O	R		D	R	U	M		A	T	B	A	T
A	B	L	E		O	O	Z	E		I	R	A	N	I
R	O	A	D	A	G	A	I	N		R	E	R	A	N
R	E	V	O	L	T	S		D	E	P	A	R	T	S
			O	A	T	S		V	O	T	E			
S	O	W	I	N	G		P	R	O	P		L	Y	E
T	R	A	C	E		S	O	A	K	S		H	E	R
R	A	T	E		O	N	T	H	E		L	E	N	A
A	T	E		S	P	A	T	S		B	E	A	T	S
P	E	R		C	A	P	E		B	O	O	D	L	E
	F	E	A	R		D	A	L	I					
P	A	R	E	N	T	S		S	I	N	A	T	R	A
S	C	O	R	N		W	R	O	N	G	F	O	O	T
A	R	N	I	E		A	U	N	T		O	U	S	T
T	O	T	E	D		P	R	E	Z		X	R	A	Y

Page 170

Sudoku

4	2	9	7	8	6	3	5	1
7	1	3	5	9	2	8	6	4
6	8	5	1	4	3	2	7	9
2	5	8	4	7	9	6	1	3
9	6	1	2	3	8	5	4	7
3	4	7	6	1	5	9	2	8
1	9	6	8	2	7	4	3	5
8	7	2	3	5	4	1	9	6
5	3	4	9	6	1	7	8	2

Mixagrams

R A D I O	P I T S
C R U S H	A B E T
S P A S M	P O L E
S N O W Y	A G E D

Page 171

Star Search

Choice Words

Follow, pursue, shadow

Page 172

Con Game

T	M	A	N		O	S	C	A	R		C	O	P	S
V	A	L	E		W	O	L	F	E		O	P	I	E
P	I	G	E	O	N	T	O	E	D		S	P	A	R
G	L	A	D	Y	S		S	W	O	R	E	O	F	F
			F	L	U	K	E			E	L	S		
E	T	T	U		P	A	T	S	Y	C	L	I	N	E
F	I	E	L	D		B	O	A	S	T		T	A	M
R	A	N		A	D	O		G	L	O		I	K	E
E	R	O		S	N	O	W	E		S	H	O	E	R
M	A	R	K	H	A	M	I	L	L		A	N	D	Y
		S	E	E		L	Y	O	N	S				
S	T	A	N	D	A	R	D		S	O	A	K	U	P
W	A	X	Y		S	U	C	K	E	R	F	I	S	H
A	R	E	A		O	N	A	I	R		I	L	S	A
B	O	S	N		F	E	T	A	S		T	O	R	T

Page 173

Go With the Flow

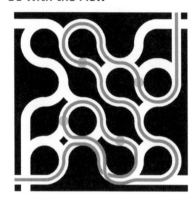

Say It Again

Grain

Page 174

ABC

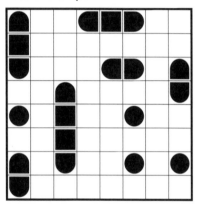

Two-by-Four

Hone, hues

Page 175

Themeless Toughie

P	A	I	R	E	D		M	R	C	O	F	F	E	E
R	U	D	E	L	Y		A	B	O	V	E	A	L	L
A	T	O	N	A	L		S	I	L	E	N	C	E	D
Y	O	U		L	A	G	S		E	N	D	I	V	E
E	B	B	S		N	O	E	L		S	E	L	E	S
D	A	T	U	M		G	D	A	Y		R	E	N	T
T	H	I	M	B	L	E		K	E	G				
O	N	T	O	A	S	T		E	A	R	F	L	A	P
			S	A	T		S	H	A	L	A	L	A	
A	P	S	E		T	E	R	I		D	A	V	I	S
B	L	E	N	D		R	E	D	S		B	A	T	S
B	A	R	R	I	S		N	E	E	D		L	A	P
O	N	E	O	N	O	N	E		D	U	V	A	L	L
T	E	N	B	E	L	O	W		A	N	E	M	I	A
S	T	E	E	R	E	R	S		N	E	T	P	A	Y

Page 176

Find the Ships

Clueless Crossword

S	C	R	I	P	T	S
E		E		I		P
C	L	A	T	T	E	R
U		C		F		I
R	E	T	R	A	C	T
E		O		L		E
S	C	R	O	L	L	S

Page 177

Hyper-Sudoku

6	8	3	1	5	7	9	4	2
7	4	1	2	9	3	5	8	6
2	9	5	8	4	6	1	7	3
5	7	6	3	1	9	4	2	8
8	2	4	6	7	5	3	1	9
3	1	9	4	8	2	6	5	7
1	3	2	7	6	4	8	9	5
9	6	8	5	2	1	7	3	4
4	5	7	9	3	8	2	6	1

Who's What Where?

A) Zimbabwean

Betweener

Tender

Page 178

Themeless Toughie

B	U	R	G	L	A	R		G	E	S	S	O	E	S
O	N	E	L	A	N	E		A	R	T	I	C	L	E
M	A	G	E	N	T	A		M	O	I	S	T	E	R
B	L	A	N	D		R	E	E	S	E		A	V	E
A	I	L	S		W	E	B	S		S	A	G	A	N
S	K	I		S	E	N	A	T	E		V	O	T	E
T	E	A	C	A	D	D	Y		R	H	I	N	E	
			E	R	G	S		K	A	E	L			
	R	A	D	I	I		E	N	S	L	A	V	E	S
S	O	R	E		E	S	T	E	E	M		I	N	N
K	U	R	D	S		U	T	E	S		C	O	H	O
A	T	A		C	A	N	A	L		M	O	L	A	R
T	I	N	C	A	N	S		E	M	I	N	E	N	T
E	N	G	A	R	D	E		R	O	M	A	N	C	E
D	E	E	P	E	S	T		S	C	E	N	T	E	D

Page 179

Fences

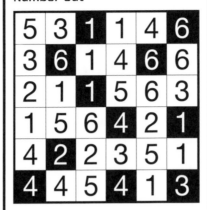

In Other Words
Cygnet

Think Alike
Below, under

Page 180

Themeless Toughie

	R	U	S	E	S		P	R	O	S	E
	S	E	N	I	L	E		R	I	P	E	N	S
D	E	S	C	A	N	T		O	V	E	R	S	E	A
E	N	C	O	M	I	A		D	E	R	A	I	L	S
L	O	U	D	E	N	S		S	T	A	P	L	E	R
F	R	E	E	S	O	I	L		E	T	H	E	N	E
T	A	R	D	E		D	E	P	R	E	S	S	E	D
			D	E	M	O	S			
A	P	P	R	A	I	S	A	L		A	G	A	S	P
C	A	R	E	S	S		T	E	R	R	A	R	I	A
I	C	E	C	A	P	S		L	E	A	P	I	N	G
D	I	S	O	B	E	Y		A	R	L	E	D	G	E
S	N	A	R	E	R	S		M	O	S	S	I	E	R
	O	L	D	E	S	T		P	L	E	A	T	S
	E	S	T	E	S		S	L	A	T	Y

Page 181

123

2	3	1	2	1	3	1	3	2
1	2	3	1	2	1	3	2	3
2	3	1	2	3	2	1	3	1
3	1	2	3	1	3	2	1	2
1	2	3	1	3	2	3	2	1
2	3	1	2	1	3	2	1	3
3	1	2	3	2	1	3	2	1
1	2	3	1	3	2	1	3	2
3	1	2	3	2	1	2	1	3

Addition Switch
557 + 428 = 985

Page 182

Number-Out

Wrong Is Right
C) bouillabaise (should be *bouillabaisse*)

Small Change
Corn flakes

Page 183

Themeless Toughie

A	T	T	A	R	S		R	E	P	A	P	E	R	S
D	R	I	V	E	L		E	X	A	M	I	N	E	E
M	A	R	I	N	A		M	I	L	I	T	A	T	E
I	V	E	S		T	R	O	L	L	S		B	A	S
R	E	S		P	E	E	V	E		S	P	L	I	T
A	L	O	H	A		D	A	D	E		L	E	N	O
L	E	M	O	N	O	I	L		W	E	E	
	D	E	P	E	N	D		S	E	R	A	P	E
		I	S	U		M	I	S	U	S	I	N	G
O	V	E	N		S	H	A	D		P	E	P	S	I
W	I	N	G	S		A	D	E	P	T		E	L	L
N	O	D		W	O	U	N	D	S		B	L	A	B
E	L	I	G	I	B	L	E		A	R	R	I	V	E
R	E	V	E	R	I	E	S		L	O	A	N	E	R
S	T	E	E	L	E	R	S		M	O	D	E	S	T

Page 184

Color Paths

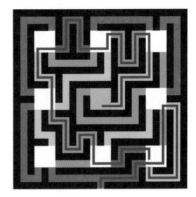

Say It Again
Bowler

Page 185

Themeless Toughie

P	L	O	W		Q	U	I	L	L		C	A	M	S
L	I	N	E		A	N	N	I	E		A	L	E	C
A	M	I	S		N	I	O	B	E		R	I	D	E
T	E	N	T		T	O	N		J	A	R	G	O	N
E	L	Y	S	I	A	N		S	C	I	E	N	C	E
L	I	E	I	N	S		G	L	O	R	Y	
E	G	A	D	S		D	O	U	B	T		A	L	A
T	H	R	E	E	R	I	N	G	B	I	N	D	E	R
S	T	S		C	A	K	E	S		M	O	D	E	M
		S	U	P	E	R		R	E	V	E	R	E
P	A	P	Y	R	U	S		E	A	S	E	D	I	N
A	C	U	M	E	N		A	L	G		L	O	N	I
C	U	R	B		Z	E	L	I	G		I	N	G	A
T	R	I	O		E	M	O	T	E		S	T	A	N
S	A	M	L		L	U	T	E	D		T	O	T	S

Page 186

ABCD

B		A	D	C	
C	B			A	D
	C		A	D	B
	D	C	B		A
A		D	C	B	
D	A	B			C

National Treasure
Norwegian